ROADIE

ROADIE

MY LIFE ON THE ROAD WITH COLDPLAY

Edited by Greg Parmley

MATT McGINN

PORTICO

Coventry City Council CEN	
3 8002 01741 938 5	
Askews	Feb-2011
782.42166	£9.99

First published in the United Kingdom in 2010.

This paperback edition first published in the United Kingdom in 2011 by
Portico Books
10 Southcombe Street
London
W14 0RA

An imprint of Anova Books Company Ltd

Copyright © Matt McGinn, 2010

Photgraphy section © Guy Berryman, Clare Bristow, Nick 'Mystic' Davies, Dan Green, Penny Howle, Carrie Levy, Matt Miller, Kit Simon, Tom Sheehan, Sarah Stockton, Kevin Tachman

Cover photography by Carrie Levy (www.carrielevy.com)

ISBN 9781907554292

A CIP catalogue record for this book is available from the British Library.

10 9 8 7 6 5 4 3 2 1

Printed and bound in Great Britain by JF Print Ltd., Sparkford, Somerset

This book can be ordered direct from the publisher at
www.anovabooks.com

To Mags, my true love, the best girlfriend and mummy alive. And our gorgeous Mary, who might hopefully read this one day and finally understand where her Silly Old Daddy Donut kept disappearing.

CONTENTS

FOREWORD

A lot of people say a lot of different things about Matt McGinn:
Brilliant axe-man of mythical origins – more egg than man,
Notorious joke-recycler,
Outrageous flirt,
Dedicated cider enthusiast.

But this much is certain:
He's been part of the Coldplay family since day one,
We love him dearly,
And at least half of this book is probably true.

Coldplay
The Bakery, November 2009

ACKNOWLEDGEMENTS

It's hard to believe in these days of ghost-written memoirs, but I actually wrote this book myself. Still, no roadie is an island – especially this one – so before we start here are some shouts of thanks and respect.

First of all, it's fair to say that *Roadie* just wouldn't have got done without the help of my nagging, cajoling, organising, editing and generally bothersome mate Greg Parmley. Right from the off, this incomparable geezer totally took the long view and made me feel that if I didn't write this book I'd be a complete twat, so I'd better just get on with it. Thanks pal. Cheque's in the post.

Cheers also to my roadie chums past and present who feature in the text and photos here, along with those who don't. No one's been left out on purpose, I've just gone where things took me. (Also, despite the sterling efforts of the fantastic snappers whose work I've gratefully and proudly included, there were almost no useable quality photos of Coldplay's vast girl-roadie team available when we went to press. Hope the snap of Vicki Taylor makes up for it, ladies.)

Much gratitude in particular goes to Jeff Dray, for taking a risk and hiring this complete rookie back in '96. Also to Nige, Kev, Kent and all at Matt Snowball Music for taking me under their esteemed, experienced wings when I first started and ever since. The whole gang at John Henry Enterprises across the street deserve a mention too, as do Mike Hill (effects and amp work), Graham Noden (guitar repairs), Joe and Flea at Vintage & Rare Guitars and anyone else that ever fixed something, sold me a plectrum or rented us a van.

Which reminds me, thanks to Ballroom, Cuba, JJ72 and any of the other bands that employed my learning-as-I-go arse back in the pre-Coldplay days, not to mention everyone that's withstood the rigours of actually being in a group with me over the years. This book might not have you lot in it but you're all part of the tale. We had some great times and no one is forgotten.

A big shout also to all those people never seen; the bloke double-driving the bus from Barcelona to Manchester; the girl who sits for eight hours guarding the back stairwell at Wembley Arena; the roadie who stops what he or she's doing to let us into the equipment lock-up . . . ta for being there, having a giggle now and then and being a vital part of it all.

Thanks to everybody at Portico, especially Malcolm Croft, for loving this idea and being a beacon of enthusiasm. Jo at Russells gets giant respect too for steering the creaking ship through the fog, as does Phil Harvey for crucial support and encouragement at the last. And much gratitude is due to Caroline Michel – wherever she is – for telling me to quit being all flowery and write like I speak. Hope you enjoy it.

To the road veterans that so kindly gave Greg and me the time to interview them: Bob Young, Scratchy Myers, Tim Butcher and Robbie Wilson, all of whom have added colour and perspective in the short bursts I've ended up quoting. Nice one lads.

Thanks also to Debs Wild and Chris Salmon at the Coldplay website, for giving me and this book a break when Greg and I both really needed it. And a big hi to Roadie 42, who – for the last time – definitely isn't me, alright?!

Thank you Rolling Stones, Clash, Stray Cats, Jam, Ash, Stranglers, Foals, Kylie, Pixies . . . the list is endless but you all made me feel like the world made sense for three and a half minutes at one time or another. Still do, cheers.

And finally, a massive, huge group hug to Jonny and the lads for giving me the best job I ever had. Well, it's a tie actually . . . working for Steve and Wendy behind the Village Inn bar at age fifteen-and-a-half is still the only thing that ever came close.

INTRODUCTION

It was tough to write this book without worrying I'd look a bit of a prize tit, especially in front of other roadies. Nothing new there, perhaps, it's been happening for years. But still, you might well ask who the hell I must think I am, exactly? And what makes me think I'm worth reading about? OK, so I got lucky, bagged one of the best gigs in the business and have managed to keep it for a long time, but really, so what? Who cares?

Well, me, for a start, and maybe even a few other people if I'm lucky. I mean, it is a pretty cool story – gluey little village punk from South Devon accidentally gets a top job in the music industry and ends up trotting the globe making a loud racket and drinking beer with his rock star and roadie mates . . . hang about, it's starting to sound like a good yarn already. And it's not just about me hopping aboard the ride either; in this tale the whole cast and core crew go from nowhere to the real, proper-sized big time and beyond, all at once and all together. Bung in a few 'A' list celebrities, an ocean of Beck's lager and enough air miles to bankrupt Branson and we're away.

I would love this mad trip to be as cool to read about – for roadies or civilians – as it has been to live through, jot down and write about. Though this book is neither a band biography (they're working on it) nor a rock 'n' roll trail of filth (go read *The Dirt* if that's what you're after) everyone – musical or not – that fancies a look inside our daft, distorted roadie world ought to enjoy the journey. It'll also probably work for anyone whose luck ever changed one day, sending them down a brand-new road to redemption, ruin or anywhere else. And there's a fair bit about Coldplay in here, as well.

OK, so maybe I need to calm down a bit. Roadie-ing's just a job, it pays the mortgage, same as anything else, right?

Well, yes and no. Every new day that I find myself out here getting paid to mess about with guitars and hear a crowd roar its approval is an absolute gift and, frankly, I can't wait to finish yacking to you lot and get back to bloody work.

My story – and, handily, Coldplay's too – is a shining example of something most folks really like to hear about. Not quite rags to riches but just the right-sized helping of fairy tale to be healthy, heart-warming and glass-slipper-fittingly unbelievable.

It's probably best summed up in as glib a fashion as possible, really. What's the word sexy old Laura San Giacomo says to Julia Roberts towards the end of *Pretty Woman*?

'Cinderfuckinrella!'

Well, how about 'Cinderfuckinroadie' instead?

That'll do, eh?

CHAPTER ONE

A ROADIE IS BORN, AND MEETS THE BAND

By the summer of 1995 my time poncing about onstage was running out and I knew it. Fun and mainly cool though they'd been, my twenty-odd years of chasing shadows through the arse end of rock 'n' roll had led me down a blind alley; I was skint, going bald and – worst of all – nearly thirty years of age. Having almost bust myself in half humping several packed trucks' worth of my own guitars and amps up and down the backstairs of every dive from Dawlish to Dagenham, I'd played a thousand songs to a total of approximately ten people and reached the same lights-on-after-the-disco-still-haven't-pulled moment that every wannabe Keef pretends isn't heading their way but secretly dreads. Seriously, there's only so far you can go on fresh air and a tin of beans. Crap deals, dysfunctional groups and limited public interest had all taken their toll and in the end the nagging, glum thought that it could be me, not everyone else, that wasn't up to the mark just wouldn't go away.

I'm not going to bore you all with too much gloomy rear-view mirror bollocks. I mean, don't misunderstand me, I had a great few years playing in bands with my pals on the whole, like most people do. But with love, thanks and respect due to everyone, I'm skipping it all out, despite the fact that without most of these other semi-desperate, die-hard people to join in I probably wouldn't have bothered, let alone found myself writing a book. Luckily for everyone, this is mainly going to be a tale of fun, joy and roadie redemption, and what crazy reader wants to wade through the early chapters of a biography anyway? You know the stuff, 'I first touched a real guitar at Mrs Bees Nursery in the village of Bantham. It was the most beautiful blue,' etc etc. Never mind all that, stop noodling and get to the chorus, man!

What might be worth getting though, since we're all here, is just how much rock 'n' roll meant to me, my mates or any other bunch of young kids coming to life in the mid 1970s. It's hard to believe now, but it was easily as big a deal back then as football was and most small boys either wanted to be George Best or Marc Bolan (or both, which was made easier by just wanting to be motorbike legend Barry Sheene instead). The shape of my whole world – like so many other kids down the years – was pretty much defined between the ages of six and twelve, during which formative period Mum came home from work clutching Roxy Music's first album and, no more or less pivotally, my long-lost Real Dad™ finally showed up, bless him. Perhaps in a gesture of extreme punk rock recompense he – and his cute young blonde girlfriend – drove me all the way to London's glorious Lyceum Ballroom in a brown Morris Minor van one snowy Christmas to see The Clash, when they were still the most fucking brilliant live group on the planet.

Ferry, Eno and the rest had already set me off but, really, it was a done deal after that night, which smacked my head, heart and wardrobe right out of the park. I didn't care which one of the Clash I was going to be, it was just a question of how.

And when.

See, the trouble with pop music is, while it becomes apparent pretty fast whether or not your name's down to win the F1 Grand Prix or score for Man United at Wembley, rock 'n' roll fantasies can drag on and on for years, even decades. There's always someone, like Strangler's drummer Jet Black or Pulp's Jarvis Cocker, who's bloody ancient when they make it and keeps your hope alive by saying things in interviews like: 'Oh yeah, you've really got to stick with it' or 'I was on the dole for forty-three summers and lived on berries from the garden.' Plus being in a band with your mates is generally such a complete blast and/or all-consuming pain in the neck that you just don't spot the time slipping by until it's almost too late to stop and get a proper job.

Before bailing, the closest I'd got to rock 'n' roll immortality had come late in the day when an advert and tape led to a kick-arse couple of days trying out on bass for the splendid, pre-shite, post-Britpop Elastica. My half-hour audition with what was then still a seriously cool outfit was so exciting and loud I could hardly believe it and – perhaps most notably – none of the band seemed to have set up their own equipment either. Effects boxes were suspiciously well taped to the floor, the bass amp was bigger than I was and the cymbals looked way too polished and shiny for that time of day.

'Ah, roadies!' I thought.

Anyway, I must've done OK as I was asked back for another tentative audition, but in the end, and reasonably enough, the lovely Justine Frischmann and co passed on me in favour of a younger, cooler and much less starstruck bassist of the correct sexual gender. The fact that their career trajectory following this choice was of a decidedly downhill nature made no odds; I was gutted. Strapped for cash and in a pretty bad mood all round, I decided things probably wouldn't get any better, downed tools and became first a cleaner, then a gardener.

No more starting blocks for me. It all seemed properly over.

Anyone who's ever lost their grip on a dream will know exactly what I'm on about. It's no big deal really, right?

Come on, do me a favour. It hurts like a bad break-up times ten. You sort of don't quite get what's gone down, even though in your heart you really do, and the idea of accepting it completely just won't compute. I'd wished I was a rock star since 1972. So why wasn't I special? How could I suddenly no longer be *eligible*? What about *all those years*?

Like many folks before and since, my plan for coping with the black clouds of disappointment and the accompanying cold, scary gut feelings was to spend a whole season of evenings and small hours as drunk as a sack. Correct living went right by me at a jaunty angle for some weeks as a raging thirst took over and most mornings became a time of real ghastliness. I must have been the most broken, hopeless gardening assistant of all time, but luckily for both me and my exasperated and equally hungover boss, things were about to take a little turn for the better.

As fluke would have it, during one pissed-up night out of a hundred I managed to stumble headlong through the big glass front door of London's tiny Splash Club and come across the fledgling Kenickie, a happening teen girl (and one boy) guitar band from Sunderland who went on to inspire fierce love and loyalty in everyone they touched, me included. I may have been half-drunk, but nonetheless the sharp, stylish, punky show I watched them give in that packed little back room struck such a resounding major chord in me that afterwards, with lairyness as my guide, I approached the two-foot-high stage to say hi to my mate Jeff Dray, who was roadie-ing for the band all on his own. Not for the last time, we had a shouty little chat that went sort of like this:

'All right, Jeffrey. Nice gig!'

'WHAT? Can't hear you!'

'I SAID, NICE GIG!'

'Cheers! Bit busy . . . actually . . . what are you doing Tuesday?'

And there it was. Just like Townshend once said to Moon. A life-changer.

For those that don't remember and/or might be interested, Kenickie – whose brilliant name came straight off the reels of *Grease* – were ramshackle and ace all at once and, unusually for a cool band, real live fantastic people too. The core songwriting team of Lauren Laverne (yes, *the* Lauren Laverne, star of radio and TV) and best mate Marie du Santiago was rooted in a deep friendship, which extended to and fully included their lovely bass player Emmy-Kate Montrose. All three sang, and though Lauren stood in the middle onstage they really were the sum of four parts, and like all the great groups they drew much of their power from something a bit like The Force, which surrounded the band members and bound them all together. Their stroppy, hilarious drummer Johnny X was, and still is, Lauren's big brother as well, so altogether there was some powerful gang magic at work – just imagine The Ramones, Nirvana and The Shangri La's in a car race after a drive-in movie and you'll get a rough idea.

Make no mistake about it, I fell so hard for this lot that my life quite literally changed course. I stopped wishing I was in The Jam and bought tools, steel boots and a box of cheap black T-shirts, having pretty much decided in the first five minutes of working for them that I was going to be a roadie or fall off the stage and die trying. I might not have been the greatest guitar repairer or amp technician in the business – I'm still not – but as Chris Martin recently pointed out to me, working really hard, making friends and getting plenty of decent backup can go a long way in this business. The fact that Kenickie's experience of road crews was quite limited worked in my favour, plus Jeff showed me a few tricks on the quiet and totally fibbed about me as well ('Yeah, he's toured with *loads* of bands', etc.) so my green-ness went pretty much unnoticed and I had space and time to learn as I went along. Terrified and exhilarated in equal measure, it was as if I suddenly had somewhere to put all those saved-up, unrequited paternal rock 'n' roll feelings and I just went at it like a proper old Superdad. Being among this bunch of glammed-up-and-going-places bairns made me so happy that when the first short UK club tour finished I burst into tears on the way back to the hire place while listening to 'Super Trouper' and nearly crashed the van. My faith in the whole point of making guitar music thus restored, I attacked the next eighteen months of my life with the joy of a golfing uncle teeing up alongside his keen, long-lost nephew. Salvation!

Sadly though, after two albums (the first of which, *At the Club*, made the UK top ten and remains forever stuffed with charm, wit and beauty) relations soured between the group's members, like they do, and it all wound up in the usual heartbreaking heap. Awful, but apt, as Kenickie's best songs always carried a little tragedy, and I watched them go with a few sad feelings to say the least. Some bands are even harder to end than bad marriages and this lot were no exception; the standard issue *Kramer vs. Kramer* period of estrangement and recrimination followed and as I was sharing a flat with Marie at the time and knew a few riffs, I ended up playing guitar in her and Em's next group, Rosita.

We were good to start with, people really dug us and during the first few vibey months I even started to think that maybe I was going to be a guitar god after all, even taking to wearing a sailor's hat onstage and everything. But despite such irresistible attributes, the most prominent of all being Marie's considerable songwriting ability, we gradually ran out of steam, money, food and everything else needed for a band's survival, before crashing gently into a wall of utter indifference. I still feel partly to blame for trying to be Malcolm Young out of AC/DC while actually looking like an antique ringer for Kojak, but in all honesty it was way too late for me really. To paraphrase Obi-Wan Kenobi's description of Darth Vader as 'more machine now than man', I had turned. I was more roadie now than musician.

It even got to the point where I was inviting my mate Adrian to fill in for me on guitar so I could leg it off on touring jobs, which I felt guilty about, but it seemed the only thing to do since I was getting too old to be so financially hard up. Rosita, who became an unhappy band in the end and eventually split, were gracious enough to let me go and luckily, all these years later, I'm pleased to say we're still on good terms.

It was during this period of transition (which took place back in what, as kids, we all used to call 'The Year 2000') that my old pal and now ex-Kenickie tour manager Jeff Dray – who'd been helping organise gigs for Rosita – was driving me home after a show one night when, out of nowhere, we had another fateful chat that went a bit like this:

'So, Matt, whatcha doing tomorrow?'

'Fuck all, man, it's my day off. Why?'

'Fancy giving me a hand on a gig?'

'Er . . . dunno. I'm pretty tired. Who is it?'

'Coldplay.'

'Eh? As in Lisa Stansfield?'

'No, you twat, that's Cold-bloody-Cut.'

'Oh yeah, sorry . . . anyway, who are they?'

'Newish band, signed to Parlophone, supporting Embrace in Blackpool. Come on, it'll be a nice earner. And besides, I'm going to be really bloody hungover so I want you to drive.'

I didn't want to do it. I was knackered from gigging, and had been dying for a rest. But it was Jeff, remember, who back in '96 had given me my first job with Kenickie. I did sort of owe him.

'All right, I give in,' I sighed. 'What time and where?'

It was one of those moments that are tiny at the time, but on looking back you realise that somewhere the Gods of Rock changed the points and sent your life off on a totally new track.

We met the next morning – Friday 5 May, fact fans – at Matt Snowball's, which is: (a) his real name; and (b) a North London rock 'n' roll storage and hire facility. For many of the old campaigners it's a gaff that's come to feel like a small fishing port; you'll always run into someone that you haven't seen since Tokyo/Paris/Tunbridge Wells and the place is steeped in a seaport-like sense of transience. I'd got there early, so had a cup of tea and chatted to the staff, a bit nervous like always when I'm about to meet new people, but totally oblivious to the significance of the coming day.

Jeff, true to his word, arrived in poor condition. He'd been up all night drinking with rural maniacs in the West Country and could barely talk, but there wasn't much time to worry as halfway through loading the van this bunch of scruffs showed up and introduced themselves as Coldplay. 'Bad hair and clothes,' I thought. One of them was sporting a debateable Paul Nicholas perm and seemed to be the leader so I thought carefully for a moment before asking him:

'So, what's the band name all about, then?'

'Ah, well now,' he replied, fixing me with the same disarming Alan Partridge half-smirk that I now know so well. 'It's the name of a special type of breeze that blows across the mountains.'

'What, like the word Keanu?' I said, before realising that somebody was taking the piss, and that the others were all having a little chortle at my expense.

'Fuckers,' I thought to myself. I was smiling though. We all got in the van and left.

A few things from that first journey up north have really stuck with me, particularly the picture I have in my mind of Chris horsing around and hoofing a ball about at a service station car park. He seemed like a big puppy, full of fun and sort of slapstick, with an immediately infectious aura that appeared to be turned up to eleven at all times. The lad made everyone on board the tiny bus laugh loads while staying noticeably courteous to the point of even thanking me for playing football with him. Guy, by contrast, gave a brooding first impression but quickly showed himself to be quite jovial and easy-going too. Will appeared solid and cool, though it soon emerged that he could swing from being quietly invisible to volubly engaging with little-to-no warning. And Jonny, who had –

and has – an even friendlier face than all the others put together, stood out for me by finding most things I said quite funny.

After a few happy hours on the motorway laughing we finally arrived at Blackpool's faded and gorgeous Empress Ballroom. The pretty chandeliers and glinting fixtures within its peeling, salty old structure set a cinematic scene for our ten-minute support-band-length soundcheck; you couldn't have wished for a better place to hear any group for the first time and even back then it was clear this little gang didn't have it in them to disappoint. People always ask me whether I like Coldplay's music and I have to say I really do, uncool or creepish as that may seem. But, as true as it is, I can't be as objective as I was on that first day when I barely knew them and they were just this odd little handful of ex-students with crap trousers.

The song they sound checked with (and therefore the first song I ever heard them play) has almost passed into folklore now and is probably just about up to speed as an all-time classic, so familiar that like 'Brown Sugar' or 'You Only Live Twice' everyone in the place already knows it before the singer even opens his mouth. Still, I won't easily forget hearing Chris's bittersweet, off-kilter acoustic intro for the first time, then the noisy bit followed by that girly, pretty verse and the spaced-out chorus-y part. It stopped me in my tracks. I thought it, and they, were great, and when the moment was right I told them. Ever the poet, I pulled Chris aside and quietly said: 'Here, that Yellow's a catchy fucker, isn't it?'

The resulting explosion of sheer glee sealed our relationship forever and set in motion a chain of impersonations that I am powerless to stop to this day. Wheeling around energetically and grabbing the attention of anyone within a half-mile radius, my new boss set everything in stone in a trice, with: 'Hey, fellas, did you hear what Matt just said?' – 'Oi vat Yellaws a catchy fucker INNIT?'

This was greeted with hilarity and universal approval in equal measure and from there on in there was no going back – whether I liked it or not, I was in the gang, and that was that.

A few weeks after that first, fateful trip, Jeff called to say that the lads needed a hand on a short UK tour supporting Muse, which turned out to be the last tour we ever did in a van . . . well, so far. At the time, Coldplay's only stage technician, sorry, roadie – a bequiffed skinny ginger geezer named Hoppy – was busy in America and could I possibly fill in? Of course I could. I already knew Hoppy (who got his nickname from a foreign landlord's inability to correctly pronounce his surname 'Hope'). We'd met on a tour back in the old Kenickie days and got on well so he rightly trusted that there was no danger of me swiping his gig.

Hoppy was, and still is, rock 'n' roll personified; a loveable, hard-working/partying rockabilly survivor of a thousand tours whose appearance actually scared the band a bit on an early encounter with him. As if a fiery red pompadour, broken denims, a deathly pallor and a roll-up cig weren't enough on their own, Hop had taken the trouble to somehow fall face first into a bathroom sink the previous night and smash himself to bits. I'd have loved to have been there to see Coldplay's expressions change when he showed up, all smiles, bandaged as though he'd just lost at Russian Roulette and looking like the world's friendliest 1950s corpse.

Muse rocked on that tour and were beginning to bite commercially as well so it was pretty exciting all round. Sold out, middle-sized gigs like Portsmouth's glass and steel Pyramid or

Sheffield's legendary-but-narrow Leadmill flew by in a whirl of newness and adrenaline, spaced out by some mad bus drives over hill, dale and misty moorland. The famous Snake Pass for instance is, on a clear day, a beauty-strewn rural shortcut through some quite delightful Pennine scenery where low stone walls, hairpin bends and random wild animals all add up to an experience James Herriot might have enjoyed. But for fuck's sake don't try it in a tour van in the fog. It'll take all day, everyone will poo their cords and you'll doubtless miss the soundcheck as well.

Some fairly pivotal arguments took place in that vehicle, which, for the uninitiated, was what we call a 'splitter', basically a modified goods van fitted with extra windows, old plane seats and a table behind the driver, plus room for the stage gear and luggage in a separate section at the rear. There's not much scope for escape or personal space in these things, tempers can flare and people quickly find out what and who they can really put up with. Chris and Guy, for example, will occasionally have a sharp difference of opinion that can easily mutate into compelling spectator sport once the pair of them get squeezed into the rear end of a cramped minibus/Learjet:

'Why do you want to call the album *Parachutes*?'

'Don't you like it as a title or something?'

'Well, no.'

'Why not?'

'I think it sounds shit.'

'Fuck off! Why are you being so negative?'

And so on.

I remember it as a happy, focused period all round though, the only real source of angst being Jeff's habit of trying to watch films on the TV screen behind his head while driving. You'd be in the back, watching Steve McQueen's car chase from *Bullitt*, when an alarming rumble would announce the fact that we were, once again, heading for the ditch. Vociferous calls from the band of 'Jeff! Stop lookin' at the bloody telly!' would usually do the trick, until next time of course.

What a circus.

Anyway, Muse's crew all treated us sweetly and the band themselves couldn't have been nicer, which was a good job really. Lots of other headline acts might have had the hump at how well their support group was going down each night and, to be fair, Jonny, Chris, Guy and Will went for the audience with the hunger and apparent confidence of James Bond or Errol Flynn, but with extra manners. Most nights, mid set, pumped up with the self-belief and sheer cheek only a true fighter could muster, Chris would address the crowd and say, 'You know, I'm not trying to be big-headed, but you really ought to make the most of this, because next year we'll be playing Wembley.'

'Cocky fucker,' I always thought, but it rang true and somehow by simultaneously playing the clown and the bard he'd get away with it. People just warmed to him, and besides, he and the rest of Coldplay made such a big, impressive noise together that you could forgive them almost anything.

Even the trousers.

CHAPTER TWO

THE BRITS 2001

Right before *Parachutes* was released, in July 2000, no one appeared to have a clue how mad things were about to get for this new indie college band Coldplay. Their record company, thinking they'd have a small hit on their hands (at best), only pressed 61,000 copies of it, though the feeling around it was good and we all thought it would at least do respectably. On the day the album came out, I bought one on CD (remember them?) at Virgin Megastore and casually enquired as to the pace of sales.

'It's been flying off the shelves, mate,' came the response. 'It's going to be number one, easy.'

'Crikey!' I thought.

After their first tour, I'd gone back to my old life of signing on, decorating people's gaffs and playing guitar in Rosita, which was fine except I was pretty much skint and clearly still not getting any younger. Next thing I knew, that new indie college band Coldplay were on *Top Of The Pops*, singing 'Trouble' with cool hair . . . well, cooler than previously anyway.

'Shit,' I thought, spluttering on my cheap home-made dole-broth, 'something's passing me by here.'

I'd heard on the roadie-vine that the band's crew was growing: as well as Jeff (and soundman Dan Green, who'd been with them almost since the off), they'd taken on Woody and Bash, a monitor engineer and drum roadie respectively, and Derek 'Judge' Fudge as production manager. Various lighting and sound technicians had been roped in too, much more of whom later.

Anyway, I was practically down to my last lentil when the phone rang. It was Jeff, saying the band needed a hand on their Christmas show at the Kentish Town Forum and could I help?

No hesitation this time. I said I'd see him there.

The days passed in a shivery, hungry kind of haze until 18 December rolled around. I arrived backstage, tooled up like a proper roadie, to find everyone jet-lagged beyond reason having just landed on a flight from Los Angeles. Hoppy and Bash smelled of booze and were fantastically grumpy, a scenario as familiar to me now as 'Yellow' itself, but quite a novelty in those early, innocent days.

Bash. As even Tommy Lee himself once exclaimed, what a fucking top name for a drum tech. Often to be found on a near-futile, kamikaze mission to out-party Hoppy and famously vague on the origins of his cartoon nickname, Will Champion's loyal onstage assistant of ten years and counting is a truly sociable, loveable gent and, having seen first-hand action on many an arduous rock 'n' roll campaign (Aussie rockers Jet's outback dive-bar tour springs to mind, among a ton of others), would certainly be an asset to any sort of rock 'n' roll gang. Myth and legend surround the past exploits of the man but suffice it to say that the sleepy villages of Middle England must be duller places since his teenage years came to a close. I'd want the geezer on my side in a scrape for certain.

Chris 'Woody' Wood seemed like a solid, professional and quite peaceful chap on our initial encounter, an impression I can't say he's done anything to spoil since. A veteran of such varied vocations as 'a bit of carpentry' and 'working for the Levellers', Woody calms us all with the faith-inspiring aura of a long-surviving ship's cat. Too many groups to list here have been lucky enough to employ him in the past as a monitor engineer but their loss has been Coldplay's decade-long gain, though at a first glance he seems to have pitched up via the sixteenth century, thanks to his long-sides-but-none-on-top hair arrangement. Calls of 'Where's yer armour?' and 'How's Guinevere?' started almost immediately and don't look like stopping. Good job he's so easy-going – the dude's as strong as a jousting charger.

So, as it was, I hadn't seen any of Coldplay since helping them out at a London in-store performance a fortnight or so before the album came out. They seemed punch-drunk and slightly dazed, which could easily have been down to fatigue, but I also suspect none of them had got to grips with what had happened since we'd last met. (They'd shifted their first ever *million records* by that point.) Before the show I asked Chris, who had a new crew cut and a wild look in his eye to match, how it felt to be strapped inside a rocket to stardom.

'Well, you know, it's OK,' he said, 'but I feel like the pilot might be losing it.'

After a tense, jet-lagged and slightly ragged show I went and found Jonny upstairs at the bar. Wondering what it must feel like to be suddenly wrenched from your shared student den and dumped without warning straight into the arms of the Top Five, I asked, 'So, Jon, you must be fed up of answering this, but how's it feel to be doing so well? Are you dealing with it all OK?'

'No one's asked me that yet, actually' he said. 'But yeah, I'm all right. Thanks.'

It surprised me to learn that he'd had zero enquiries thus far about his wellbeing, but there we are. I felt a little bond between us started in that moment, but I don't suppose he'd remember it as, not for the last time, we proceeded to get properly wankered and spout rubbish on hot topics such as the greatest riffs of The Pixies and our favourite sorts of girls, which little did we know we'd soon be doing a whole lot more of on the buses, planes and backstage docks of the world . . .

The following February, about a week before The Brit Awards, Derek Fudge rang. Speaking in his best Stephen Fry-via-Watford telephone voice, he asked, 'Dear boy, I wonder whether perhaps you might be at all interested in keeping an eye on Guy and his bass equipment during the live performance of "Trouble" at the Brits?'

Diving at the chance without any trace of grace or dignity, I got my shit together and days later showed up at Earls Court with a little tool case, which I'd painted 'Coldplay' on just to be trendy.

U2 were receiving their lifetime achievement award that year, so we all got to watch them rehearse, which for an old fan like me was total schoolboy stuff. I didn't meet them, but encountering The Edge's guitar technician Dallas Schoo for the first time was a real treat. We got along well and, though I was a bit overwhelmed to be in such esteemed roadie company, I remember liking the way he coiled up his cables and thinking, 'That's good, I'll nick that for later.'

To be honest though, compared with the rigours of doing a proper show, the actual workload turned out to be a bit of a doss. Hop was in charge of Jonny, Bash did the drums, while Derek helped with Chris's piano, but there was really very little to do in those days as the backline was dead simple, not much more than you'd need to do a tiny pub gig with Chas 'n' Dave. I set up Guy's amps, stuck them on a rolling riser (a little mini-stage on fat castors for any non-roadies still reading), tuned the bass guitars and just got on with soaking it all up, worming my way in and trying to get as popular as possible. Nowadays, having hung around TV studios for more hours than I've drunk bottles of Beck's (I may well have miscalculated this), there's still the same excitement but far less of the teenage wonder I felt back then at suddenly being allowed access to such a top level. So much of it all just made me dizzy: big lights, bulging cameras, presenters you recognise from the telly and, best of all, loads of pretty, clipboard-carrying young women running around in black outfits and headphones.

It was a top night, at any rate. Coldplay won two awards for best band and best album, one of which ended up on Derek's hotel sideboard the next morning, though he still says he doesn't remember how. I immediately noticed how good the band had got – 'Trouble' sounded crisp and powerful and really worked in the slightly supper club-esque surroundings and a whole new audience was born, and smitten, inside of three minutes.[1]

The best thing, mind you, about anyone's first awards event is always the free booze and star-spotting. I'll never forget how the entire backstage bar – celebrities and all – stopped on a dime when Kylie walked in, or the hilariously imperial figure Robbie Williams

---

[1] I'm still pretty convinced that this was partly due to the fact that moments before show time Chris decided that he liked my light-blue, roll-neck sweater and was going to have to wear it on the telly. Fame at last – well, from the neck down at least.

cut as he strode for the stage flanked by shaded heavies. (Kylie actually watched Robbie's performance on our TV but I was a bit shy of her, not like later in this book.) Eminem was about as well, in a killer mask and carrying a chainsaw. Anyway, after the show we loaded everything back into a big van and that was that. It was actually a big surprise to me that we didn't have to then go with the stuff and put it all away the same night, like you do on some small gigs, which gave me and my new colleagues time to hang about and bond a bit over fairly large amounts of complimentary alcohol. Some slightly surreal stuff went down backstage, like Brian out of Westlife striding into the dressing room in full stage make-up and a blue leather jacket with no agenda other than declaring his love for *Parachutes* to anyone who would listen. And more seriously, Steve Lillywhite, a man whose production work we'd all been loving (consciously or not) for years, completely choking me and Chris up outside in the corridor by citing – in front of his kids, mind – Coldplay's music as a major force in healing the scars left by the tragic death of his ex-wife, their mum, Kirsty MacColl.

We all rolled home a bit drunk in various cabs. (Tour buses were yet to become an integral part of my everyday life, though I wouldn't have long to wait.) All in all my whole first Brits experience had pretty much blown me apart and, like the moment I decided I was going to roadie my arse off for Kenickie or die in the attempt, the whole night made me realise that sticking with this special, unusual little band was absolutely the way forward.

CHAPTER THREE

BACK, BACK... AND BACK (AGAIN) IN THE U.S.A.

May 2001, just off the flight from Heathrow to Boston. Worn out and pretty thirsty, me, a small crew and three band members trooped into the bar at a mid-priced Swissotel, wondering what the hell would come next for us all in this huge, scary new world. Chris, having arrived a few days ahead of us, was sitting on a sofa all alone in big rock 'n' roll sunglasses, looking like something had changed.

We got drinks, huddled in the snug around him and after the first happy greetings someone piped up and asked how he was doing.

'Well, fellas,' he said to everyone stone-faced, 'I've been thinking. We can really do it in this country, y'know?'

Fuck me, I thought. He's bloody serious.

During the months following Coldplay's success at the Brits, my life had returned to something like normal yet again, i.e. eating cheap pasta, smoking roll-ups and trying to make the rent. I was busy painting a wall for extra cash when Derek rang and calmly altered the entire course of my life. For the second time.

'Hello, LW, everything all right?'

Piss-taking fucker, I thought. 'LW' stands for 'Lieutenant Worry', a title he'd coined himself that I can't really dispute, as anyone who knows me will testify. I'll fret about anything from global catastrophe to whether my boots match.

'Yeah, not bad, Del. What's up?'

'Well, dear boy, I might have a little job for you. Are you busy?'

Little job. He wasn't kidding. Five weeks with Coldplay in North America, on a make-or-break jaunt across the entire continent. I said I'd think about it.

Days later, having decided that the decorating could wait, I found myself landing in a whole new world. Big trucks, proper posh buses, and loud, experienced American crew members were suddenly all around, making me feel like Christopher Columbus and a little lost sheep all at the same time.

Ask any English roadie who's toured the States at any level and they'll tell you it's not an experience to be taken lightly. Suddenly, the rules change and the goalposts aren't even goalposts any more, they're bloody ballparks. You start meeting the kind of people who are actually *in* famous songs, such as Derek's temporary Canadian replacement Jodi, who turned out to be not just any old Jodi, but Jodi as in the line, 'Jimmy quit, Jodi got married' from 'Summer Of 69' by Bryan Adams.

This sounds daft, and it is, but it's the kind of stupid stuff that starts making you feel a bit odd and weirdly exhilarated if you even slightly give a shit about pop music. All over the US you're constantly running into sights and places that dive straight at you out of the most celebrated tunes of all time, and at first it can really knock a freshman roadie sideways. For instance, I spent my first day off in New York walking around agape because every other sight, street or road sign seemed to have been immortalised in a song by Lou Reed, Frank Sinatra or the Ramones. And, if you've grown up in the UK watching imported American telly, it's game over – the whole country will seem amazingly familiar and yet utterly surreal, as if you've stepped out of a dream and onto a film set. It's no wonder so many groups get there and just go completely mental. I mean, how are you supposed to concentrate on navigating the American pop marketplace when you feel like a kid who's just landed a bit part in *Starsky and Hutch*?

Good question. With which – and any virgin roadie's stateside wellbeing in mind – here's Matt's Top Ten US Tour Tips:

1) Make the flight. Unless you're Hoppy, who somehow managed to show up at one US gig on time even though he was still in bed while the rest of us were checking in at Heathrow.

2) Try and alter your attitude to jet lag and see it more as a subtle shift in workable drinking time.

3) Talk louder, as if you're having a chat with Fozzie Bear.

4) Get along with local crews wherever possible. (If you don't have any signature picks, Krispy Kreme doughnuts usually do the trick.)

5) Learn how to queue at embassies, airports, CVS pharmacies etc.

6) Get used to weak beers. Or hit the top shelf.

7) Eat plenty of burgers and get your new, massive 'butt' stuck in the bus aisle, between the galley and the 'can'.

8) Remember, your English hair-clippers/electric-toothbrush

/drill/personal sex toy won't work on 110 volts.

9) Under no circumstances hint at any dislike of Cheap Trick in a public place.

10) Don't panic. There's always somewhere open that'll sell you cigs, beers, Trojan condoms, beef jerky etc.

Not many British groups manage to 'break' North America, for a variety of reasons. Some, like say The Jam or Blur, ultimately stall because their artistic currency is a bit too English, preventing mass US audiences from 'getting it' (though The Kinks did all right in the end, which kind of stiffs my case a bit). Others might suffer from poor managerial/label support, or – on actually being faced with the sheer scale of the task in hand – a sudden, incurable bout of plain old can't-be-arsed-itis. It's a long list, which could take hours in the pub to unravel, but the few groups that do make it there share one common characteristic. Great gulfs of stylistic and musical difference arguably separate Def Leppard, U2, The Beatles and, now, Coldplay, but there's one unifying factor: none of them went over and pissed the Yanks off by being lazy, arrogant twats. You can say what you like, but all these bands did essentially the same thing, which was work like dogs, charm everybody silly and, most importantly of all, acted as though they actually wanted to be there.

Doing this doesn't come naturally to everyone, which is understandable, as there's a lot about the American music business that gets on some English folks' tits. For instance, the hellish round of 'meet and greets' (also unfavourably known as 'grip 'n' grins'), in which groups are required to shake hands and be chummy with every local industry rep and music-biz type – quite often straight after a performance – can seem too phoney to bear. But at the end of the day, it works both ways, and like anybody that's being chatted up, Americans like to be wooed properly.

And, if you're going to woo anyone in the States, make no mistake about it – you'd better woo the hell out of the radio stations.

It's easy to forget that the USA is absolutely fucking massive. (It can take between five and six hours to fly coast to coast; God knows how anyone got across it in a wagon.) And it's full to the brim with live regional FM radio stations – 13,750 at the last count – many as important to the area they cover as Radio 1 is to the UK. If you wanted to make any impression whatsoever back in 2001, you simply had to get these people on your side or no one was going to hear you, and it'd be time for an early bath and bedtime. In the years since, the internet has obviously gone silly and changed everything, but for Chris, Jonny, Guy and Will taking their first American steps back then, getting heard there at all meant playing at what are known as (whisper it) 'The Radio Festivals'.

These are dreaded events for any new group. Imagine a blazing hot midsummer's day at an oversized outdoor sports venue full of bad hair and worse armpits. You're one of a ten-band, all-day outdoor bill, shoehorned in between Linkin Park and Green Day at 3 p.m. in front of 50,000 rock fans who, at that time, wouldn't have known Coldplay from their own arses (sorry, 'asses'). Despite the odd great moment, like in Foxborough, MA, when the revolving stage spun too early while we roadies were still up there tuning and the previous act (an unknown bunch of keen, tanned and shirtless skater-boy types) were still tearing into their final song, resulting in a hilarious side-stage punch-up involving them and the local stage crew, you've really got to fear the worst. A certain amount of proto-emo/metal mutha hostility towards a bunch of limeys playing nice songs with keyboards was to be expected in those early days, but it didn't make things any more fun. Hoppy and I actually got coins and bottles thrown at us while we were setting up the gear one sweltering afternoon at Washington DC's gigantic Patriot Center – I thought, oh no, we've even got black T-shirts and tattoos and they *still* hate us. What's going to happen when they see Chris's bloody piano? Rumbles of disquiet filled the packed stadium as we nervously tuned up the light-brown acoustic guitars.

The moment Coldplay appeared, a predictably massive wave of negativity seemed to sweep towards the stage, threatening to wash us all away forever. Rock-steeped, hot and grumpy as hell, the band's newest audience just weren't having any of it and the majesty of 'Yellow' and prettiness of 'Shiver' just melted in the afternoon heat and evaporated, borne upwards on a cloud of sweat and jeering. I felt that at any moment some unseen, leather-clad hand would pull a secret lever and we'd all fall through a great big trap door straight back to London.

It was during 'Trouble', though – perhaps the gentlest song some of the crowd had heard since 'Nothing Else Matters' by Metallica – that the pivotal moment arrived. A sense of mutual purpose gripped the particularly furious section closest to the stage as soon as they heard the now-familiar pretty piano intro; luckily a large barrier was preventing them from carrying out the massacre they had in mind, which only served to compound the atmosphere of condensed hatred for the band. If anyone in the place was enjoying the show we had no way of telling and midway through the second chorus it happened: with the skill and purpose of an ancient warrior, some little joker thirty rows back launched an uncased CD in a precise arc which hit Chris right on his sweat-drenched, reddening forehead.

'I never meant to cause you . . .' CRACK. It was that perfect, and tragic. You had to hand it to the thrower, who'd clearly played in the high-school music-media projectile team for years, and if Chris had got up, pitched something back, called them a load of wankers and gone home on the next flight I wouldn't have blamed him in the slightest.

But he didn't. He just sort of stiffened, looked at Jonny, kept on going and leaned hard into the storm. The band held fast around him, kept it all together and survived, suddenly looking to me like a proper little fighting firm.

'Nice one,' I said to myself, feeling like Mr Kincaid off *The Partridge Family*. 'These kids are tougher than I thought. Maybe they're going to crack the States.'

I wonder what CD it was? Probably not *Parachutes*, but you never know. Still, the moment summed it up for me; it was the first small victory in a series of successes that saw Coldplay take it right to the top of the world's biggest market – not bad for a bunch of 'ex-students in crap trousers' (er, who said that?). Step by step, mile by mile, state by state, the small entourage crunched its way back and forth like a polite, hard-working platoon; clubs, then theatres, then national TV . . . *Saturday Night Live*, Conan O'Brien, Letterman and Leno all fell for this funny little gang who by now we were all fiercely loyal to and protective over. We soon became known as the loveliest crew in the world, but we didn't fuck about – there was, and still is, a steeliness lurking behind the smiles that partly comes from the band and the feeling they put into us. (Not to mention the fact that we're really just a bunch of typical grumpy roadie bastards pretending to be nice.)

Whatever, it was a good blend of characters that saw us through some absolutely crazy scheduling over the next few years, which, by the time *Spin* magazine named Coldplay their Band of the Year 2003, had really started to pay off. As top *Spin* staffer Tracey Pepper wrote at the time:

> [*A Rush of Blood to the Head*] has sold 9 million copies worldwide – 3 million in the US alone. As the lukewarm success of fellow Brits Blur, Travis, and Stereophonics has proved, breaking America can be a struggle. To ensure that they wouldn't go the way of their compatriots, Coldplay crisscrossed the continent six times from May 2002 to August 2003, performing 155 shows – in small towns like Bend, Oregon – and glad-handing endlessly. 'We whored ourselves around,' [Chris] Martin admits. But the prostitution paid off. By the time they played sold-out shows at the prestigious Hollywood Bowl and Madison Square Garden in June 2003, Coldplay had transformed themselves from Radiohead obsessives into a critically respected, celebrity-props-receiving mainstream sensation.

Radiohead, my arse. But you can see her point. We were off and running.

CHAPTER FOUR

GLASTONBURY 2002: THE BIGGEST SHOW OF OUR LIVES

Before flinging themselves headlong into the arms of America, there was still some serious business for Coldplay to attend to back home. It was towards the tail-end of recording sessions for the band's pivotal second album, *A Rush of Blood to the Head*, when people started to get panicky, and not without good cause. The lads had been booked for some months to headline the first night of Glastonbury, but things had taken longer than expected in the studio and the album wasn't going to be in the shops in time, simple as that. I'd been helping them out here and there with equipment deliveries, setting up gear at Parr Street Studios (Liverpool) and Air or Mayfair (London) on a kind of piecemeal basis while taking on other odd jobs to fill in the gaps, so I'd built up a fairly objective outsider's-eye view of how the recordings were going.

The general vibe in the Coldplay camp around this time was basically like a mixture between squaring up for a scrap and running for the bog. There was no way these lads were going to back out of a challenge but at the same time they were understandably bricking it about how the new record would be received by the world at large.

It seems funny now, since 'The Scientist', 'In My Place', 'Clocks' and all the rest are loved the world over and seem like they've always been there, but you have to remember that when the future Biggest Band In The World™ started work on this stuff they'd still had fewer actual hit records in the UK than Travis or The Stereophonics. As if the idea of following up something as popular as *Parachutes* wasn't scary enough, the band was now faced with a tough choice – cancel the Glastonbury show and play it safe, which would disappoint everyone (not least of all festival organiser Michael Eavis, a fan, friend and champion of Coldplay from the very earliest days), or bite the biscuit, do the gig and pray to the gods of rock 'n' roll that everyone would break with tradition and go mental for the new songs on first hearing.

And I really do mean everyone. Apart from the massed legions of paying folks actually in attendance, plus all the other groups and crews on that day's bill, huge amounts of people would be watching on telly or reading about the show in the papers over the next few days, deciding amongst themselves if Coldplay were good or crap, and whether or not to buy their records. All things considered, this would not be a show to fuck up.

It's a fair measure of the daring and sheer thirst for victory at the heart of the band that they didn't plump for an easy life. With Creation Records boss Alan McGee's infamous 'indie bedwetters' barb doubtless still ringing in their ears, the band decided to show some bollocks and step right up to the oche.

First things first, then. A fortnight's rehearsal time was booked at The Depot – a cavernous, prison-sized (and sadly now defunct) space near London's Kings Cross. For the band, putting together the Glastonbury set in advance meant learning *Rush of Blood*'s new tunes and getting good at them, which this time around also involved working out how to keep in time with the violins and other extra noises that were discreetly playing along on backing tapes. Add on a ton of other niggles like what the lights were going do in 'Clocks', where the drum kit should be positioned onstage or how many verses 'Everything's Not Lost' had before the end sing-along bit and you'll start to picture the size of the task.

For me and the rest of the crew, rehearsals are a chance to iron out technical hitches, learn what guitar goes where and drink tea for cash. Sometimes things can get fairly intense, especially if someone in the band reckons it's all sounding shit, but on the whole rehearsing is a largely pleasant affair not too far removed from the act of getting all the toys out and having a few mates over. Still, there's only so much you can achieve in a soundproofed, audience-free room, so the idea was hatched that we'd head off on a little warm-up tour. Four shows were swiftly arranged, each one in or near to the band's respective childhood stamping grounds.

I remember clearly the sheer, full-on head rush of the first night in Aberdeen at a small hall seating a few hundred Scots, who as a rule are always noisy and up for it at gigs. We were well prepared, but the sense of collective relief among the crew when 'Politik' struck up for the first time was nevertheless pretty obvious. For those who missed what became the *Rush of Blood to the Head* tour, the tune was a storming opener which Chris has since confessed was designed solely with their debut Glastonbury headliner in mind – all crashes and slashing chords lit up by flashing, almost blinding, white light, which stuck fast for a year and a half as an unstoppable overture. I was stunned, but still managed to shout, 'Wow, that was pretty cool!' to Jeff Dray by my side.

He stayed silent. Good sign.

The rest of our jaunt called at a few slightly larger venues in Liverpool, Bath and Truro, and was good fun all round, apart from my first really embarrassing technical cock-up in front of a couple of thousand Scousers. Not content with handing Jonny a wrongly tuned guitar for his performance of the fledgling 'Clocks', I later managed to drop a blob of superglue into one of its vital moving components mid-gig, rendering his favourite Fender Thinline Telecaster temporarily useless. Nice work, roadie!

Things other than industrial-strength adhesive were actually falling into place though. By this point all the core team had got some fairly big shows behind them. We'd already supported U2 in front of 80,000 people at Dublin's Slane Castle the year before, and most of the newer crew boasted some sort of large outdoor concert experience. The Coldplay roadie gang started to knit together more and develop a sense of unity, anticipation and common purpose. The work was challenging but really satisfying so our off-duty beers flowed nicely and the laughs came easy – you just couldn't help but be excited. Still, underneath the camaraderie, everyone on board, band included, was all quietly shitting it about the looming festival. And before we knew it, it was upon us.

Jonny has said of his first bill-topping Glastonbury show day that it's the most times he's ever been to the toilet during one period of being awake. Everyone else in the touring party was displaying various symptoms of high anxiety too – normally a beer would do the trick, but no one wanted to be fuzzy round the edges when show time came around. Having arrived the previous night and done as much onstage setting up as we possibly could[2] there was nothing much to do except hang around the festival bar or on the tour bus, not drinking, just getting more and more tense. In the end I simply couldn't handle being around my jolly, relaxed pals or any of the crew any more and finished up walking about the site worrying on my own for hours, which of course didn't help in the slightest.

I've been moaning about festivals for years, ever since my mum dragged me to Hood Fayre (a mini Glastonbury near where I grew up in South Devon) aged fifteen. My new monkey boots got fucked in the mud, there were no bogs and I ended up around the campfire playing bongos all night with a bunch of ethnically dressed, stoned hippy bastards just to avoid the falafel (the real hot dogs ran out about teatime, surprise, surprise). To be honest, I've never really got over it, and even now there's an element to festival life that really gets on my punk rock tits: dust, muck, buskers, clowns and vegeburgers are all great things in their place but there's something about sticking them all together in a big field . . . I dunno.

We've done a thousand festivals since, though, and I've learned to love and appreciate them for the good bit – the bit it's all for, that immense moment when the stars collide and the amazing, cheerful, people (who, let's face it, aren't getting paid and don't have a bus full of cold, free beers and nice bogs to poo in) jump up and grab it with both muddy, happy hands. It's amazing when it arrives for real, but right then it was following me around the site, bugging me like a fucking lost juggler.

'What? No, I don't know where the Bumfields are, mate, leave me alone!'

---

[2] Bash reckons he'll never forget line-checking the drums. 'I couldn't believe the size of the site,' he says. 'It looked brilliant.'

A few hours of this kind of public-spirited, inclusive, party behaviour brought me back to the catering tent and a little supper, followed by the usual flossing/brushing and a stiff trot back up to the stage area to growl at people some more and recheck the equipment.

Nerves, man, bloody hell. Perhaps I need to learn some useful calming techniques. Maybe I ought to smoke a bowl or two and hang around the big stones more often. Seasoned production manager Derek Fudge has always said, quite rightly, that, 'It's just a concert, dear boy. It's not life or death.' But, to revisit the famous words of legendary soccer manager Bill Shankly: 'I can assure you, it is much, much more important than that.'

OK, he was talking about Liverpool Football Club, and possibly half-joking, but that's pretty much how it feels when there's an hour to go, 100,000 people are whistling and baying in the summer night air and you can't get one sound, not one note, out of the guitar rig. This was the state of affairs in my corner of the world by 9 p.m. so, feeling a bit lost at sea, I shouted to Chris Martin's roadie for help.

'Hoppy. It's fucking broken. What am I going to do?!'

Luckily, my good friend and colleague, who would have probably fancied popping out for a quick pint during the Blitz, had a look and nonchalantly noted that I'd plugged it all in backwards. Phew!

You get about thirty minutes (or more if you're really special) changeover time between bands at most festivals, which is pretty much the same as a normal show, but there's a crucial difference. At your own concert, most things are left in place and all you have to do is remove the support band's equipment, shift a few bits about, plug in, turn on, and go. Headlining a bash like Glastonbury involves a different sort of discipline – whole lighting towers, big screens and huge backdrops have to be wheeled into place and tested during that half-hour window, while the drum kit, amplifiers and piano come in on rolling risers. It doesn't just have to work either, it's also got to be safe, and when you stop to ponder the amount that's going on, it's quite amazing that more people don't fall over, bump their heads, break stuff or even blow themselves up. But, generally, most shows seem to get started on time, everything does what it says on the packet and, more often than not, nobody dies.

Building a show this size, in limited time and with enough onlookers to start a small city, is about as exciting as it gets for a new roadie. The energy and adrenaline levels are just daft, right off the dial, but somehow you have to keep solid, focused and composed – if you rush it you'll forget something, or trip, and there really isn't the time. So Hoppy, Bash and me are stood on or near our respective risers, wound up tight like pre-pounce cats, clutching the instruments as if clinging for dear life to skinny drainpipes. Everything has been pre-tested offstage and all of the amps, keyboards and drums are ready to be pushed out by us and the massed, black-clad, local crew; the last synthetic washes of Faithless's set melt away, the stage is cleared, the back curtain rises and – holy shit, we're up.

I'd never seen a crowd that size from a stage before. It looked more like a weird, multicoloured pre-harvest prairie than a field full of people. About twice the turnout you'd get at most big football games stretched back to the horizon, half-lit under the night sky by torches, fast-food stalls and cigarette lighters. It was chilly for June, and you could see your breath in the air. Coldplay were due to take the stage at any minute, and the whole audience – excited, sun-damaged and, in all likelihood, tipsy at best – was doing a good impression of a mad, massive dog straining at its leash. Probably the most celebrated annual outdoor event in the history of rock 'n' roll,

Glastonbury looked and felt for all the world like one giant Jack, just waiting to be unboxed.

I don't get to see the band just before they come on, I'm too busy tuning up offstage to the right and hoping I've switched everything on properly. I know the lads always used to have a psyching-up group hug though, and sometimes I see them approaching the stage, their path lit by various dudes with dim, blue torches. The shadowy, silhouetted scene nearly always looks the same: Chris bopping like a boxer while the others compose themselves nervously around him. It's an almost sacred time for them, knowing that any second the lights will go down, the crowd will explode with delight and there'll be no turning back. The responsibility we have to get it right for them all at this moment is huge and it's pretty cool to feel so trusted.

Standing in the wings to the right, surrounded by Jonny Buckland's arsenal of guitars and sound equipment, I felt scared and right out of my depth. Scaffolding, lights, video screens and huge speakers all swayed and towered up into the darkness above me, seeming to say, 'Matt McGinn. You're much too small. What the fuck are you doing here?'

Good question, I thought. Maybe one day I'll answer it.

Chris has said that he still can't believe Glastonbury 2002 really happened, claiming – not unreasonably in view of the sheer stress levels involved – that he doesn't remember playing the show at all (save for a feeling of trying to get through it) and would love to go back, do it all over again and actually enjoy himself. The others talk of a 'huge adrenaline buzz' and being 'gobsmacked' by the light show, while Jonny says his only real recollection is of looking up at the vast, green lasers for the first time and allowing himself to think – finally – that he and his friends might just have pulled it off.

Woody says he doesn't recall a thing until afterwards when he found himself standing on a rainy loading dock, wondering what the hell had just happened. Hoppy has no recollections whatsoever and Mystic's not even sure if he was there. Derek remembers feeling close to tears as he watched the lads tearing into 'Yellow' that night; apart from the joy, pride and relief, he also recalls being blown away by the sight of the entire audience lit up – right to the back – with masses of extra yellow lights that the lampies had brought in specially and stuck way out on the front-of-house tower.

Bash's Glastonbury '02 experience was, sadly, defined by the receipt of some terrifying news – at 10 a.m. on show day, the call came through that his beloved mum had suffered a bout of meningitis so severe that it had put her straight into a coma. After a good deal of soul-searching (the band actually offered to send him home in a cab) his father told him to stay put as it was his big day and it's what she would have wanted for her boy. Happily, 24 hours later Mrs Bash came round – with, miraculously, no lasting physical damage – and went on to make a full recovery.

For my part, once the band finally hit the stage that night, it's mostly a total blank, just gone, deleted, wiped forever. I can picture so much more from our headline slot three years later (the flags in the crowd, the beautifully timed, crowd-driven Kylie tribute), which is frustrating all round, since normally my long-term memory is such that I'll know exactly who said what to who, where we all were and which pair of jeans I had on. Sad to say, the only two things I now properly recall about the most crucial concert of all our lives are:

1) 'Politik''s intro – the perfect hello, like a surprise slap on the back – lifting the band and crowd together while simultaneously thumping Alan McGee over the head; and

2) Getting a big, proud feeling inside me that everything was working and – thank fuck – we were going to be OK.

Strange thing is, I do remember some daft things about the aftermath, like my triumphant post-show rock 'n' roll cheese, pickle and crisp sarnie washed down with the mandatory chilled Beck's and – in those days – umpteen post-show cigs. Meanwhile, though, the band was stuck in the grip of a mini-nightmare – a simmering hell's broth of euphoria, frustration and claustrophobia apparently took hold of their tour bus as it got delayed in the festival muck by warring gangs of armed nutters slugging it out beyond the perimeter fence, causing our sweaty, half-mad and probably itchy heroes to see dawn well before any sort of soap. Ugh!

I've since watched footage of Coldplay's first Glastonbury headline performance and it's actually a lot less wild than their shows became later on in the tour, when the madness had really taken hold and the wind was right in their sails. But all the same, that night, for all our fears and hopes, and against massive odds, the band cracked it and the crowd rolled over.

Things would never be the same again.

CHAPTER FIVE

WHAT'S A ROADIE ANYWAY? PLUS: THE WORST GIG OF MY LIFE

'The first credential is you've got to be fucking barking mad.'
Robbie Wilson, Slade roadie, 1970–76

In his otherwise sharp and funny personal memoir *Cider with Roadies*, ex-*NME* hack, writer and broadcaster Stuart Maconie arguably does his book's fantastic title a disservice by hardly talking about roadies at all until right near the very end, and then only giving us about a page and a half of jocular but stereotypical and, truth be told, rather sketchy insight. It's a bit like *Tubular Bells* – completely absorbing and daft throughout but with fuck all actual tubular bells until the last bit, then it goes slightly out of tune for a minute, Sally Oldfield starts singing and that's the end of that.

Well, no worries – I knew about roadies already and much preferred reading stuff about Wigan Casino in 1974 or what Morrissey was like to interview. Still, as Basil Brush used to say on telly every Saturday when the storybook snapped shut for another whole week: 'B-b-but . . . but . . . you can't leave it *there*, Mister Roy!'

Cider with Roadies is great. But if you *really* want to know all about us, stay here.

OK, for a start, some roadies refuse to admit they're even 'roadies' at all, and call themselves something else, like 'technician', or its abbreviated form 'tech'. This is understandable, as during parts of the last few decades some sections of the road crew community – not to mention their employers – behaved with such disregard for respectability that the already murky name of the profession was properly soiled. Tour buses and hotels became known as places of ill repute; healthy and decent behaviour dropped way down the list of priorities and certain lowly substances became almost as common as Golden Wonder crisps.

The folks who participated in or witnessed any of this might argue that it was all harmless fun, and I'm not here to point the finger. It's just rock 'n' roll, right? As long-time Motorhead roadie Tim Butcher rightly points out: 'The reason people went to work for bands in those days is because they wanted birds, booze and life on the road. They didn't want to do the nine to five. Today it's vastly different – everybody's a super-qualified technician but a lot of the fun's gone out of it.'

Depends on your idea of fun, I guess, but you can see his point. All the same, the upshot was that the word 'roadie' came to mean 'smelly old crook of no fixed abode', and it's kind of stuck. I suppose it's true that there are (and probably always will be) plenty of blokes who want to give out backstage passes to pretty girls in the audience and get off on the whole retro Led Zep trip – that's up to us, er, I mean *them*, and the bands they work for – but most other crew members aren't like that and just want to be out there getting on with the job. No, really. Honest.

Like I said earlier, this book isn't going to be a trawl through the filth, decadence, fun, gloom and all-round pioneering insanity of popular music's vile, hilarious past. Sorry, but any true student of rock 'n' roll will tell you that great tomes and a whole host of lyrical waxings have already spewed forth from the fried memory banks of many a more qualified reporter than me. It's fair to say as well that the pickings are probably a bit leaner these days, compared with, say, the complete carnage of the late 1980s LA poodle scene or even the moddy-fied cokefest that grew out of good old 90s Britpop. Seemingly, the backstage/tour bus world of today is, despite the sterling efforts of a few young scamps and one or two scaly old warhorses, getting to be a scarily professional, competitive arena and really you can only party so much before . . . pardon? Did someone say 'lightweight'? Yeah, I know. I should try going to work for Lemmy, get 'em in, rack 'em out and grow some fucking bollocks, right?

Well, hang on a minute. Coldplay crew members, like the band themselves, don't just wheel out the bloody Horlicks and the board games post-show; we all like a good knees-up with a pint and a pie after work, same as anyone else, though we haven't yet gone to the lengths Status Quo did in the mid 70s.

'We had a club for a couple of years, with membership cards,' says Quo collaborator and former roadie Bob Young. 'We'd get a suite in a hotel, take all the booze in there after a gig, get all the pot plants from around the hotel and set it all up. It was so we didn't have to go out to clubs after the shows – we just brought all the girls and the dealers and the madness back to the hotel instead. If anyone was out of order, they could lose their membership. The drummer was thrown out by security once and barred!'

And some funny shit still does happen. You know you're in deepest tourland when someone suddenly and rather aggressively declares the back lounge of the flash yet cramped bus their 'office', only to be walked in on mid-shag/blowjob/game of Scrabble by a hapless colleague who wasn't aboard when the new rules came in.

All harmless and highly amusing, but lately I've found it pays to just chortle from a safe distance – though it's easier said than done on a wild night when the juice is flowing and laughs are aplenty. For a start, I'm fucked if I can do my job hungover any more. It's all right when you're twenty-five but get ten or more years down the road and gigs of any size just start to hurt too much, especially when the loud cheering and horrid cymbals get started. Plus, though it's not very rock 'n' roll to say it, a lot of us have partners, kids, mortgages and other sundry loves/responsibilities to think of and, though it's nice to be off the leash now and then, you've really got to look out for and after yourself.

In our job it's all too easy to take advantage of the whole daft night-time bubble. This is especially true at the posh end of the gig business where to get close to the band is, for some fans, a prize worth any price, but plenty of folks simply aren't into all that stuff and think it's old hat and slightly naff. I'm lucky, I work for and with people to whom common decency is a high priority, which in itself tends to attract and encourage exactly that. I'm proud, not ashamed, to call myself a roadie and always do, much to the amusement/ horror of those who might somehow feel the need to disassociate themselves from the unwashed and the unseemly.

But still, just renaming ourselves 'technicians' doesn't automatically make us become all nicely scrubbed and savoury, does it? Call this life of ours whatever you like but I'm sure I'm not alone in wanting to reclaim the 'R' word as a positive term and revive it, with good associations attached. Our line of work is – on a good day – a skilled, professional concern, and to me, 'Guitar Roadie for a Massive Rock 'n' Roll Band' sounds like the coolest job title in the world.

So what do us lovely, clean, professional-minded people actually do for a living? And how did we all get started? Is there a warm, safe college course available with a tasty little crew qualification dangling at the end of it?

Well, OK. For a start, yeah, there are now courses, good ones too, run by people who know their stuff. Sadly though, applying to the University of Rock wasn't an option for me and my school chums – we all left class in the 1980s when further education was for proper students and most of Madness were still under thirty. Bizarrely though, since bagging the Coldplay gig I've actually spoken at the Brighton Institute of Modern Music as a (check it out) 'guest expert', the very idea of which made some of my mates titter only slightly more than I imagine the college kids did as I walked away.

Still, the real question is, in the absence of such scholastic opportunity, how did a teenage pain in the arse like me – or any of my current peers, come to that – turn failed exams, crap school bands and serial solvent abuse into an actual job? Where's the way in?

Well, finding it – like rockin' a rhyme that's right on time – is tricky. Often roadies start out by accident, like our ex tour boss and old chum Jeff Dray, whose career in road management followed a few low-level but enjoyable bass-playing posts which, it's worth noting, he made easier for himself by assuming early-doors that the three thinner strings on his guitar were only there as 'spares'. Fate came a-calling one fortuitous night when he fell asleep on 80s hair-band Dogs D'Amour's tour bus and didn't wake up until Manchester, whereupon being spotted by the crew, Jeff was gently encouraged to make himself useful by carrying something heavy into the venue. Somehow, in that split second, the lad promptly discovered an innate organisational bent and a talent for barking at the enemy that have since seen him, and others, through many a tough touring campaign.

By contrast, sometimes a childhood event might lie dormant for years and subconsciously trigger a whole life's work, such as in the case of well-known lighting mogul and raconteur Bryan Leitch, who once said to us all on a tour bus travelling through North America: 'I remember as a kid accidentally setting fire to my parents' curtains at home. The whole lounge burned fiercely for some time before anyone noticed, and I was too transfixed to move from the spot. I thought it looked absolutely incredible.'

Coldplay's keyboard and gadget man Matt Miller, never one to miss a jape, replied, 'So now you make lights flash and smoke bombs go off for a job?'

The chap looked stunned, and confessed that – amazingly – the connection had never occurred to him.

But really, if we're all honest, a lot of roadies – and I include myself in this – are simply the failed musicians, freaks and misfits that school couldn't help and *Top Of The Pops* didn't want. Some are bitter: I know roadies who hate bands and are completely jealous of their employers but just can't bear to tear themselves away. Others are genuinely helpful people who know it's only rock 'n' roll, but still like it, and don't want to go in for their tea just yet.

Personally, seeing bands like The Clash as a kid made me think rock music made some kind of pure, powerful, basic sense and I count myself lucky that I still feel like that nearly thirty years later. Sometimes I catch a youngster in the front row watching me tune up before a gig and it reminds me how amazed I was when, as a seventeen-year-old Jam fan, I realised that Paul Weller had at least one spare guitar up there and, better still, someone to change his broken strings for him! I also remember how cool and kind most of the crew seemed, so now I always try to be as generous to young fans as The Jam's employees were to us. You want Jonny's sweaty towel? Here it comes! Plectrums? Fucking catch, then!

Quoted in Paulo Hewitt's 1982 biography, *A Beat Concerto*, long-serving Weller road boss Ken Wheeler had this to say on the subject:

> The Jam realise that touring is about the kids and they've always stuck to that. It even got to the point that when the band were onstage and there was a couple of kids by the stage door you'd pull them in. The band put that sort of feeling into you . . . I've told people to fuck off and had a right bollocking from Paul.

That said, there are times when you can't help getting a bit testy, especially after a hard day's night when people are shouting for souvenirs and showing scant signs of courtesy or respect. Granted, all of us, crowd and crew, might be a bit overexcited by that point in the proceedings, but nonetheless. If anyone reading has a friend who's about to go to a concert anytime soon then, please, politely ask them not to call out any of these things towards the stage, pre-gig:

1) 'HEY, ROADIE!' OK, I know I said I liked it, but this is really annoying, especially in certain accents. Fuck off, I'm busy, and it's Mister Roadie to you, all right?
2) 'PICK!', 'DRUMSTICK!' or, most often, 'SET LIST!' Sorry, but no. Where are your manners? Go away!
3) 'DON'T IGNORE ME, YOU WANKERS, I'VE COME ALL THE WAY FROM . . .'

You get the idea. We want to be friendly and give everyone prizes if they are nice, so why not try these instead:

1) 'EXCUSE ME?' That's better. Or even . . .
2) 'EXCUSE ME, SIR?' Lovely!

Some Coldplay fans actually know what we're called and beckon to us by name, hoping for treats, which can be flattering or a bit freaky depending on how jet-lagged or paranoid we all are. Either way it'll get our attention for certain and is rarely unwelcome. The only time we'll ignore somebody that's being polite and persistent is if we're under pressure to clear the venue for security purposes, in which case anyone onstage dishing out gifts might easily get told off for causing a delay/fights amongst the punters. At the end of the day though, those old-fashioned punk touring ethics still serve us all best, as summed up neatly by Clash DJ Barry 'Scratchy' Myers:

'I would never make out that we were all good boys and nobody was interested in the perks of the road, but one thing that was important in the Clash camp was how you treated your fans, male or female. It was a reaction to how other bands had previously treated people. We weren't puritans, we still liked to party, but it comes down to that notion of respect.'

Ask someone who knows and they'll tell you how much all our jobs can differ from gig to gig. (In fact, the sheer variety of tasks and skills involved in keeping any type of show on the road is worthy of its own massive chapter, so I wrote one – it's called 'Gig Day' and you can skip ahead to it any time you like.) I always think 'Guitar Tech' is a bit of a misnomer, to be honest – a good chunk of my job has nothing much to do with actual guitars at all, like dealing with crazy effects units, electronic switching, busted amps, tour bus politics, travel burn, extreme fatigue, hangovers, etc. It really isn't enough to just be a bit handy with instruments, though that definitely helps; for example, some roadies are fantastic technical people who you'd kill to have around even though they aren't especially musical, while others – like me – have come at it from a background of playing in groups which, while not being especially scientific, brings with it its own set of useful experiences. I always try to imagine what I would have wanted myself if I'd had a roadie of my own, and then just throw it all into the pot. I'm lucky too in that there are five or six experts I regularly call on for help and advice and can usually learn something from, even if the next day I'm scratching my shiny bonce and thinking right, which way round did he say the red wire went?

Lots of musicians, core staff and visiting crew get along together just great, but some of the best/worst stories you'll hear come from people who've got the hump, such as one case in which a well-known roadie actually stuck his index finger a full half-inch into an onstage cameraman's non-filming eye. The victim, it seems, was guilty of a cardinal sin we all recognise on the road, namely totally ignoring us and getting in the way even when asked twice not to, and it's safe to say he probably didn't do it again. Personally, I've been pretty lucky over the years – I've only ever felt like pushing one especially mouthy little prick off the stage and into his own audience, which in the end no one actually needed to do as the kid pissed so many other people off along the way that he kind of buried his own career. But if you're going to go for it and try to have your own set of roadies, remember they're not all as soft and cuddly as me.

Success levels and differing budget sizes bring their own special variations to a tour too, meaning for instance that quite often newer or less-established groups need crews to multitask a bit, like in the old days before steam was invented. Robbie Wilson (Slade) talks about sold-out, 1970s heyday tours being done in Avis furniture vans and Volvo estate cars with three roadies and no security whatsoever, on wages of less than twenty quid a week apiece – hardly a king's ransom even then. (This would be the sort of deal you'd expect when starting out with a fresh, unknown band nowadays, not a massive act that's wiping up dough with a sponge and appearing on telly more often than the weathermen.) Touring of this sort can be tough, rewarding work if you're part of a useful team, or complete ball-breaking misery if not. It's often great fun on the way up when everyone's hacking in there, the mood is good and even though there are only eight of you aboard – including the talent – it's all right because you're all heading for the toppermost of the poppermost and even the bassist doesn't mind doing some of the driving. As Motorhead's Tim Butcher remembers: 'Everybody, including the band, got up and we all worked to get the show set up. It didn't matter if you were lighting, sound or backline, you just helped out, then we'd all go down the pub until soundcheck!'

Most roadies of a certain age have worked on tours a bit like this and I'm sure lots would agree that when it's all running smoothly things can be just lovely. The mad, bad stuff usually happens at the other end of things when an act is just about to run out of puff and everyone's getting desperate, throwing in daft routing and corner-cutting ploys that save cash but could get you into some really treacherous scrapes. Like, for instance, one job I did years ago saw me and another skint skinhead taking endurance and sheer bloody-mindedness to new levels by getting behind the wheel of a splitter-van, driving all the way to bloody Rotterdam, setting up a gig, playing, tearing everything down, packing up and then hauling it all back to London in one hit to save on hotel bills. I can barely remember the journey home but I know we shared the task and that I drove part of the way so fucked it wasn't funny.

The point is we didn't *have* to do it. But the show must go on, right? We're roadies. We're broke. It's a challenge. No matter what, we're going to make the gig happen.

How totally stupid.

By contrast, at Coldplay's current level every crew member is well looked after and usually has a specialist job, me included, although as well as being Jonny's exclusive axe butler I've also been known to play live on a couple of tunes over the years – hidden away out of sight, obviously, to stop the lasers bouncing off my gleaming head and completely spoiling the show. The first time I was invited to become a secret rock star was for a packed house at Belfast's 10,000-seater Odyssey Arena – which at less than a day's notice you could say was a bit scary – as midway through the 18-month-long picnic, also known as the *Rush of Beck's to the Bus* tour, Chris Martin suddenly decided he wanted to climb around the venue a bit and generally act more like a rock-star mountain goat. It was mid-afternoon on the day of the show when he fixed me with his trademark 'Here's A Challenge, Are You Man Enough?' look – a panic-inducing and unavoidable half-grin that comes to us all if we spend enough time around him.

'Matt,' he said, placing a fatherly, you're-fucking-nicked-son hand on my shoulder. 'You have to play my acoustic guitar parts on "Yellow".'

Bloody hell.

'Oh, er . . . OK. When?'

'Tonight, please. Offstage, though. Do you mind?'

'Um, no. Course not. How does it go?'

'I'll teach you. Let's do it.'

'All right.'

Eek!

We retreated to a small, spookily yellow side room and soon discovered to our mutual dismay that because my thumbs were (and probably still are) two thirds the length of his, I was totally incapable of playing his awkward chorus parts. Oh dear. A tense, testing minute and a half passed before my Pub Rock Emergency skills kicked in and saved me from failure as all those years of churning out impromptu, non-negotiable requests at violent rural hootenannies came to fruition. The sight and sound of battling Young Farmers and Hell's Angels barking orders at whoever's been mad enough to clamber up onto the tractor trailer with a guitar soon teaches any quaking musician the ultimate simple truth, which reads precisely as follows:

If a song's playable, it's playable using Status Quo Chords.

Don't laugh, I know what I'm talking about. Try dishing up anything even slightly cerebral at a remote, unpoliced motorbike rally organised by crazy, oily bastards and see what happens – you'll get a riff and a half in before they request some 'fucking rock 'n' roll', which you'd better have a stab at, or else. Not a dissimilar thing to learning 'Yellow' in a hurry really, except I doubt Chris would smash your guitars and set your van on fire if you failed.

Coldplay know all about this kind of stuff, as it happens. They've done a few boozy gigs of their own and are actually bloody good at them, if their secret charity set at North London's Shepherdess Inn back in late 2001 was anything to go by. Introduced on stage (well, pub carpet) by actor, friend and regular customer Simon Pegg, the band – minus a poorly Guy – started things off with a sort of request-tune tombola. Things went along pretty nicely at first as the crowd were treated to some gentle, pretty versions of 'Trouble', 'Don't Panic' etc., until, a few songs in, some pissed gonzo over near the bar suddenly went, 'OI! DO "LIVIN' ON A PRAYER"!'

Er, sorry?

'"SWEET CHILD O'MINE, COME OOONN!"'

This is what happens when you play pubs; people drink beer and demand 80s FM radio classics. There are three ways to deal with it:

1. Keep playing your acoustic ballads, stare at your feet and hope the hecklers will go away
2. Tell them to piss off, thus starting a massive fight, or
3. Say, 'Listen, don't try and be funny, if you want to hear it then we're going to fucking play it, OK?'

Looking back, this might have been the moment something snapped inside Coldplay, making them want to be a huge, sports-venue-

The Duty Prefects second gig, Clare's party, Kingsbridge, South Devon, 1980.
Proof that nothing lasts forever, especially if you keep bleaching it.

See what happens?
Me with the lovely, 75% hirsute Rosita, Finsbury Park,1999.

Early days, late nights. Guy joins the roadie party, *Parachutes* tour, 2000.

'So, when are Aerosmith gonna show up?'
Dan, me and Hoppy get an early feel for stadiums, Foxborough, Massachusetts, 2001.

Roadies off-duty. L-R: Jeff Dray, Hoppy, me, 2004.

'Hang on, who's roadie-ing for who here?!'
Mayfair Studios, London, 2003.

Right ... 30 degrees without prewash for this load, I think.

'Ah, the perfect hiding place!'
Will Champion turns a blind eye…

'D'you know, I'm feeling a bit homesick.'
'What are the chords?'

Hoppy.

Woody contains his excitement during line-check, *Viva La Vida tour, 2008.*

When dealing with lippy musicians, even the cuddliest roadie has a limit.

Exasperated musician wonders how many more years he'll have to endure his
roadie's crap jokes. Loyal bandmates chortle politely, as cover.

Who says blokes can't do three things at once?
Izod Center, New Jersey, 2008

'Great crowd tonight...'
Izod Center, New Jersey, 2008

shagging, zillion-selling global concern for real. Chris, Jon and Will immediately stiffed their own back catalogue and tore right into the stadium rock cover versions like they totally loved it, but with jokes, which worked so ridiculously well it now makes you wonder if they might consider bunging in a bit of Bon Jovi next time we're at Wembley. The show climaxed with a rousing 'Yellow' and a hilarious rendering of 'When The Saints Go Marching In', featuring what might be the earliest known public airing of Jonny Buckland's deep bass 'Concrete and Clay' style backup vocals. The smartarse twat heckler went home, not realising he'd indirectly changed the future face of arena rock and the small, tipsy audience proceeded to go completely bananas while me and my roadie pal Neill got so excited we drank ourselves sideways and had to persuade nearby girls to help pack up afterwards, because we couldn't see.

Anyway, back to the story. Once I'd found the Quo way around 'Yellow', Chris went off none the wiser and I was left with an empty room, a guitar and . . . fuck me, stage nerves. Since becoming a roadie I'd almost forgotten how horrible these little bastards can be – imagine extreme exam panic but mixed in with one of those bad dreams where your trousers won't stay up at school and everyone's staring at your bare bum. And, nerves or not, it's quite a responsibility starting off 'Yellow' on guitar when an arena full of people has paid good money to hear it. The true enormity of the scenario only hit me once I'd stopped looking at the guitar a few gigs later and cast my gaze away towards the crowd.[3] You know, those chiming, familiar acoustic guitar chords that signal the song's arrival? When the

---

[3] OK, so I'd already been playing soft chords on half of 'The Scientist' since the tour started but if I'd dropped the bat during that song, who would have really noticed? Playing 'Yellow' was a totally different kettle of fish, as I had to play the actual intro.

audience goes absolutely mental? That was me, for a year, every night, off the stage and in the dark, bricking it in case I accidentally played a jazz chord instead and made the whole crowd go 'Eh?' instead of 'IT'S YEEEELLLLOWWW!!!!' (which, incidentally, I never did, all right?).

Mind you, just have a go at playing the last minute and a half of any tune, simple or not, while the lighting crew are doing a strip tease in the wings to put you off. If you're any kind of decent person I'd like to think you'd do exactly what I did in Columbus, Ohio, and totally unravel with mirth, mangling the pretty little ending bit so badly that it rendered Guy helpless with laughter. Obviously we were all sacked immediately after the show, but how sweet to be the centre of attention!

Still, it's not duff notes or panic attacks that really keep roadies and live musicians awake at night. It's something else, something almost too scary to mention. I'll see if I can describe it for you . . .

As far as Jonny and I go, we haven't had too many technical disasters, although anyone who's done this kind of job for long enough will have at least one nightmare tale to tell. Whether it's Twickenham with The Rolling Stones or Arlene's Grocery with Dave and The Shitheads, every guitarist, singer and roadie is at the mercy of hundreds of wires, one of which will – sooner or later, ready or not – decide to snap. And snap one really did in Belgium. Holy shite.

We'd been on the road promoting *Rush of Blood* for about twelve months and were beginning to feel invincible and slightly insane in equal measure. By the time our party reached the backstage area at the 2003 Rock Werchter festival, millions of records had been sold and every gig was packed while the band and crew were beyond confident and had become used to concerts being either fairly good or just totally unbelievable, as if it was a normal life we were all leading. I wouldn't say I was smug but I'd certainly started to think I was one of the big boys as I merrily chatted away to R.E.M.'s crew backstage, blithely unaware of what the gods of rock had in store for me and my poor old trusting boss Jonny Buckland.

The aforementioned Mr Matt 'Milly' Miller has a theory that life on the road accentuates everything, including the power of old adages. So, a worn-out saying like 'Pride comes before a fall' could hold whole new reserves of significance in the context of a concert. This came frighteningly true when, three songs into the triumphant, still-daylight, nowhere-to-hide show, Jonny's guitar sound cut out completely halfway through 'A Rush of Blood to the Head' – just silence – in front of 30,000 people. Including R.E.M. And their crew. Who were all standing right behind me.

Fuck. What now?

OK, first off, was it the guitar or the cable? Checked them. No. Plus, it looked like there was what we call 'signal' – i.e., the electrical impulse that represents the guitar sound – getting through the whole effects system. But no noise.

Fuck again, but with added Oh Jesus.

Maybe it was the amplifier itself – checked that too, but no, another dead-end, the amp was fine.

By this time the song was half over and I was thinking I'd sack it and go to the spare rig, which at that time was basically an emergency baby version of our main setup. I suggested this to my rapidly reddening boss who agreed that, yes, it would save time and aggro. We waited until the tune stopped and gave it a go in the gap.

It didn't work either.

Who's seen *Jaws*? That bit near the end where Richard Dreyfuss's character Hooper is submerged in the shark cage and – aargh, dork – accidentally drops his pointy stick into the deep just as our great white plastic villain begins to bend the bars with its snout? I won't spoil the ending for anyone left in Christendom who's still yet to see the film, but there's a look of horror on the actor's face which, even without the diving mask, you'd have recognised on mine that day in Belgium too. Put simply, I was fucked.

I went through everything again and checked what I could but the fact is I was utterly bamboozled. And when things are that wrong and you've spent three whole songs trying to claw it back, you're going to be way behind and ill prepared for anything else, least of all joining in on 'Yellow'. It was truly tragic, and in the end being so lost and out in the open caused Jonny's record-breaking fuse-length to desert him. Wearing the mask of a wronged Welsh dragon, he kicked over the spare amp in a rage, causing it to almost land on an unsuspecting young camera assistant who was hiding behind it. No harm done, but Jonny was immediately upset and very concerned; onlookers said they'd never seen a facial expression change so quickly.

We limped feebly through the last part of the show making some sort of noise, although I don't really remember how or what. All I recall is a blur of effects pedals and cables, and that hot, tearful, lip-chewing sensation that only accompanies true failure and embarrassment. The band, thank the Lord, just got on with the gig, held things together like proper professionals and ensured that we all got away with it. But me and JB were badly stung forever.

Of course, the next day, we uncased everything backstage, plugged stuff in and couldn't break the rig if we tried. I've since come up with ideas about what happened that seem feasible – duff connections, broken plugs, poltergeists, etc. – but in the end we'll never really know. An entire duplicate setup was quickly flown in from our American arsenal just in case, although the rest of the tour passed without further incident and – touch wood – it's never happened again since. But still, we'd learned a valuable chant, which is worth knowing by heart if you're ever thinking of doing any sort of serious roadie-ing:

Don't start thinking you're cool because that's when things blow up.

And, most importantly of all:

For fuck's sake, if you can afford it, have three of everything.

CHAPTER SIX

STARS AND WHITE STRIPES

I've always been starstruck, ever since I was a little kid. I remember when I was about nine – before I switched to learning the electric guitar – my drum tutor Vic got a gig playing for Val Doonican, a popular, middle-of-the-road Irish singer who had his own TV show in England in the 1970s, which my nan and I would watch together most Saturday nights. Nearly always smiling and/or twinkling, Val wore nice, cosy sweaters and often sang from the comfort of a large, white rocking chair. Though I never got to meet him, I sat down one day and, just for fun, rewrote the lyrics to one of his more popular songs, which Vic kindly forwarded. I've still got Val's polite, encouraging and personally signed reply, and even now – thirty-five years later – it makes me smile whenever I see it.

To be honest, despite being among famous folks a lot in my job, I haven't really changed. Just when I think I've got used to it all, someone like Madonna will walk past, reminding me how fucking bonkers life around here can really get sometimes. Once Kylie Minogue popped by the Coldplay studio during the *Viva La Vida* sessions and I just happened to answer the door to her, which was weird in itself, but only until I realised she was completely up for a massive flirt. It was all a bit cheeky like the school corridor for a few minutes, but in the end I had to go on errands, or something, and she was scheduled to do some vocals with the band so I quit while I was ahead and excused myself by saying, 'Hey, Chris, I'm off out, if you don't need me for a bit . . . well, unless the lady needs tuning or anything?'

This produced gasps of glee all round, not least from Ms Minogue herself, who spun right round on her cushion and exclaimed, 'Well, stick around, I might!'

I'm not always this cocky, though – it depends on the type of star and what they've ever meant to me, I suppose. And you can sometimes really take yourself by surprise; I didn't know I even still gave a toss about Stewart Copeland and Andy Summers until I saw them getting off a plane three decades after blowing me away with 'Message in a Bottle' and clammed right up when Copeland walked past, smiled right at me and said 'Hi'.

Another time I held the door open for Paul Weller at the BBC, when I was doing Jools Holland's *Later . . .* show with Kenickie. Not much of a story, granted, but I was suddenly a speechless fifteen-year-old Jam fan again, and couldn't wait to tell my pals (his gruff, totally satisfying 'Cheers, mate' will probably go with me to the grave). The next time we spoke was a good ten years later when, just moments before the old geezer's acceptance of a Brits' Lifetime Achievement award, my lovely girlfriend (who'd been goading me all night, bless her) virtually pushed me into his path where, feeling like a totally shagged rabbit, I spluttered a bit of teen idolatry worthy of . . . well, me in about 1981, to be precise. But, good on him, he took my hand, shook it and doubled his previous word count with a clipped but cool 'Fanks very much, man', seemingly quite chuffed that I'd made the effort. And the night I met Eddie Izzard, well . . . my jokes are shit, as anyone will tell you (like you hadn't noticed already). But all the same, I made him laugh with some poorly realised gag or other and it was as if Keith Richards had got off his cloud and come down just to say, 'Nice guitar riff, Matt.'

I know. Pathetic, isn't it?

The most embarrassing thing that can happen though is that you run into someone like The Edge and accidentally say, 'All right, mate?' as if you know him. (The only way to make yourself feel more of a tit than this is by shouting out 'Mum' in class instead of 'Miss'.) These people are as familiar to us music fans as our own reflections, and it's all too easy to forget that The Edge wouldn't recognise me from, er . . . Adam.

It's quite weird to spend time around people you've admired, even worshipped, from afar. Sometimes they are as lovely as their tunes, which is always a relief. Jack and Meg White, for example, were all sweetness and light; I met them both thanks to a random call from Matt Snowball's just as 'Fell In Love With A Girl' was breaking the band wide open in the UK for the first time. These were the days when people were still frothing away about whether this wild-sounding duo was an ex-married couple or actually brother and sister, but I wasn't bothered about all that. They just seemed like a couple of cool, odd, nice kids in funny outfits who were excited and grateful to be doing what they were doing. Meg was diffident but very sweet and gracious while Jack – who had a sort of big-guy confidence and star quality about him even then – politely engaged me on all sorts of topics we shared a love for (guitars, which Stones album was best, etc.), even though all I really did was fill in at the last minute for their normal roadie by driving a van around London for a couple of nights, tuning two guitars and setting up what was then a brutally simple onstage backline rig.

Other stars can be a big disappointment, and almost put you off their terrific music just by being twats, but we'll mention no names here. Worse by far are the times when you end up meeting folks whose tunes are so awful they make you want to eat your own legs, and then the bastards turn out to be REALLY NICE PEOPLE. Many's the terrible band I've been forced to start liking because of this and, trust me, it really fucks with your sense of personal integrity. Nothing you can do, though. It goes with the job.

But really, oddest of all is when you start working for a band who only Steve Lamacq, Parlophone Records' A&R Department and a few thousand indie kids have ever heard of, and two years later cabbies are saying, 'I 'ad that Chris Martin fella in the back of 'ere the other night,' except, of course, Chris doesn't gets cabs, he travels by yoga. But you see my point. If you've ever been even slightly impressed by celebrity, you can't help: (a) being freaked out; and (b) totally loving it, when your mate and boss gets properly famous. Some of the best fun you can have is walking around with a well-known chum on a good day, when the attention is friendly and unthreatening and the kids are alright. Once at Dublin's Witnness Festival (now known as Oxegen) I had to pretend to be Chris's second bodyguard and walk through the crowded site with him and our then head of security, a largely sweet but bloody scary dude who it's safe to say probably didn't need my help. I've experienced some moments of feeling pretty important doing this job, but striding along getting stared at while trying my damnedest to look really hard was one of the best. I felt like Dolph Lundgren for the rest of the day and it was fucking ace!

Not like the night Liam Gallagher rounded on me backstage at Oasis's Roseland Ballroom show in August 2002, mistakenly thinking I'd squirted him with a water pistol, when it was actually a daft girl stood in the corner that did it. The conversation went like this:

Liam (coming towards me looking a bit mental): 'Ey, ey, ey! What the fuck was that, man?'

Me (backing up like a total sissy): 'No, no, no, mate, it was her over there!

Things all got a bit nuts around the time that *Rush of Blood* really started to bare its commercial teeth, particularly in the USA. People like Rachel Weisz and what's-her-name from *The X-Files* began turning up backstage after gigs, Elton John did a guest turn onstage in Atlanta (to some of the loudest applause any of us had ever heard), and one night after a high-rolling show at The Hard Rock in Las Vegas, I even encountered Spiderman star Tobey Maguire in the hotel elevator. The potential for shite gags in a situation like that is obviously enormous – like, 'whatcha doin' in the lift, dude? Lost your powers?' etc. –, but all I could manage in the event was a breathless 'Fuck me. You're Spiderman!' which actually went down quite well. (I invited him to join me at the bar, but he said he was tired and off to his room to surf the 'web'. . . bloody hell, sorry.)

Another big hoot was my first foray into the rarefied, star-and-entourage-studded world of LA's Chateau Marmont, a high(ish)-end hotel for rock gods and media big shots on Sunset Boulevard often used by regular music-biz types. Dimly lit, the bar area was mellow, hushed and had a couple of stairs down into it. I spied Will and

Jonny chatting to Minnie Driver (who, I noted from the top step, is even hotter in real life) and Michael Stipe (ditto, pretty much) on some fancy big sofas and thought, cool, I'll just glide on over and join in, real suave like. It didn't turn out quite like that. I went over on my arse down both bloody stairs yelling 'FUUUUCK!' at the top of my voice and spilling booze all over the poncey carpet, bringing the whole room to a big, silent halt. Well, what do you do? Get up, go outside like everything's normal, smoke a fag and feel like a complete dildo, that's what.

And then, just when you thought it couldn't get any madder and you were allowed to start feeling normal . . . crikey on a bike, Chris fell in love with Massive Amazing Hollywood Movie Star™ Gwyneth Paltrow.

The boys in the crew had – sorry, boss – been speculating about who the new lady in town was for weeks, and of course there'd been a few shady snippets in the media about it, but until she actually started showing up on the tour no one really knew for certain. Luckily, I wasn't totally aware of Gwyneth's work or quite how famous she was when we were first introduced, or I might've been a bit more stunned, what with me still being starstruck over Val Doonican and all. As it happened, I was stomping around scowling in my roadie costume (black T-shirt, jeans, big boots, knife, dirty fingernails, torch) hunting for something before a show, when I burst into a side room and there she was, just sitting on a table. 'Bloody hell, it's her,' I thought. Chris wasn't there, but Jonny was, and I can still clearly recall our first conversation.

'Matt, this is Gwyneth,' Jonny said. 'Gwyneth, this is Matt, my roadie.'

'Oh, hello, how do you do?'

'Hey, nice to meet you,' she said. 'Are you the Matt that plays guitar on "Yellow"?'

Wow, I thought. A proper actress has heard of me.

'Yeah, that's right.'

'Well, it sounds great!'

Bless her. I was lost for a moment, so – for better or worse – I decided to act cocky, since the only alternative would have been to go bright red in the face. It was a big gamble, but I went with: 'Cheers. So, d'you think I play it better than your boyfriend?'

Thank fuck, it hit the spot; she laughed and so did Jonny. Afterwards I felt a bit guilty for throwing a nice compliment back in her face, and said sorry a few days later, but she brushed it off and asked, 'Why are English guys always apologising?'

Obviously when I got home and saw my pals again for a pint, one of the first things they asked was, 'Well then, did you meet Gwynnie? What's she like?'

Yeah, I did. And she's great. Just a normal girl, really. Well, except for the rock-star husband, y'know?

Like I've said, Coldplay weren't always a massive commercial and artistic concern. When I first got involved with them things were quite different to how they've now become, in all kinds of ways. But really, for me, half the fun of being part of their journey has been in noticing the little markers along the way – those daft occurrences that just make you think, 'Oh good, the lads got a little bit bigger today.' Like them all being invited to Sunday lunch at Bono's, for instance.

Jonny and Will told me that the morning after supporting U2 at their colossal Slane Castle show a few years back, they both awoke wondering if they'd dreamed it, so one rang the other's hotel room just to check. No, it was true, they *had* gone to U2's party, and yes, the lead singer *had* said, 'Come to ours for a roast tomorrow, lads. And don't worry about directions, ask any cabby in Dublin – they all know the way.'

Despite being mortally hungover and in some pain, our two nascent stars decided that it was all too *Jim'll Fix It* not to make the effort and – fantastically – the driver of their first hailed cab on St Stephen's Green was no disappointment, taking them straight to Lord Vox's front gate without so much as a raised eyebrow.

Us lot, i.e. the crew, were all sat with a few ales at the Fitzwilliam Hotel bar when Jonny and Will returned some hours later. They'd had a lovely afternoon and were made to feel most welcome, which is nice, but not the point of the story. What's great to me is that I remember thinking, 'Jammy little bastards. They've been to bloody Bono's house. How cool is that?'

A little tickle of excitement rippled along the bar, like we'd all just walked through a new, previously locked door together – the first of a great many more, as it turned out. It was as if suddenly, and finally, after years of separate struggles, being involved in music was beginning to do all of us a favour.

It's funny how nowadays the lines have blurred the other way and the markers are starting to look a bit distorted. I mean, a lot of Coldplay's support acts of recent, *Viva La Vida*-related times have included some quite big names – not like U2 big (imagine that, what a scoop), but people like the lovely Duffy and her entourage or Albert out of The Strokes, a nice young chap with a sweet band who all acted like everything was amazing the whole time and couldn't stop thanking our 'awesome' crew for 'looking after us so nicely'.

Well, cheers, but we were just a bunch of old knobheads from England last time I looked, mate.

Truthfully, we've had some splendid acts out with us over the last few years, most of whom have turned out to be great people as well. The list goes on and on and, when it's working, having a cool support band on the road with you can be as much fun as a new special friend coming to stay over. I remember for instance some hilarious impromptu post-gig bongo jam sessions with northern spaceheads The Music, who, it's fair to say, were quite partial to the odd late-night recreational cigarette.

And touring with the mighty Ash was like a dream come true for me – they supported us across the States in 2002, at the height of their powers after *Free All Angels* had gone huge in the UK, and were simply unbelievable, musically, socially and professionally. These people (and front man Tim, in particular) never dropped the ball or sulked *once* even though: (a) they were touring America in an SUV with all their gear in a trailer; and (b) despite these valiant efforts, the USA, on the whole, didn't seem to give a shit. Night after night Ash turned in a world-beating, Coldplay-baiting show and still only a cool few ended up knowing who they were. Still, imagine my excitement – after years of adoring Ash from afar – at being asked to stand in on guitar for their delayed leader at a soundcheck one afternoon in Baltimore. It truly was roadie's playtime as I surprised the band by chasing them through an almost flawless *Kung Fu* on Tim's Gibson Flying V. Fuckin' sweet, as the singer himself might have said, had he been there.

Rilo Kiley were a nice bunch of lads and one lass who backed us up for a bit during the North American *X&Y* shed run – or *Twisted Logic*, as the tour was officially called. Linchpin singer and multitasker Jenny Lewis grabbed all our attention right from the off by being extra cute, well turned out and really good, but nonetheless I couldn't help noticing a guitar just like Jonny's being played by one of the group at their first soundcheck. Covered in tools and wearing my best roadie frown I clomped over to the moustachioed young man in question and said, 'Nah, mate, you can't play a vintage Thinline on our tour. Jonny's the only one allowed, he's got a special deal with Fender.'

For a moment the whole ensemble fell for it, including gag victim Blake Sennett, who later confessed to me he'd accepted my ridiculous ruling swiftly enough to comfort himself with the notion of using his other axe instead!

We've even had a few massive, properly big league acts like Alicia Keys and Jay-Z around, or even on the same bill at some events, which calls for a different sort of roadie decorum entirely. I mean, it isn't a contest, but let's be honest, these people are total showbiz royalty that even Chris is in awe of, never mind little old me. I usually find a blend of complete respect and sheer cheek gets pretty good results when dealing with such huge names, like when Jay Z's whole twenty-strong entourage plonked themselves right in my way five minutes before a Coldplay festival appearance up in the mountains outside of Vancouver. 'Props' to the 'massive' for reacting politely and positively when yours truly piped up thus: 'Er, 'scuse me, Jay, can you all move to one side, mate? I don't want to twat anyone on the head with a guitar as I'm going by.'

Best of all, though, I was once forced to choose between Alicia, her two minders and the backstage corridor wall as the three of them approached me at a clip, right after she'd done a wicked guest spot on 'Clocks' in some utterly incredible silver legwear. The heavies puffed up and looked like they meant to crush my sorry arse but you've got to have some fun, right? I puffed up back, looked right at her and put forth a cheery, 'Nice gig, Alicia! Cool trousers!'

'Hey, thank you!' came the upbeat, smiley reply. Not only gorgeous, the lady's gracious as well.

So, how does it happen? How did Alicia Keys get from Hell's Kitchen to the top table? And Jay-Z from Marcy Houses Projects to Madison Square Garden? Or how about Chris Martin? What twists and turns sent him from rural England's prestigious Sherborne School to right up alongside these two huge forces in American music?

And, more to the point, how the fuck did all four of Coldplay become so bloody successful?

If I could provide definitive, easy answers to these sorts of questions I'd bottle and flog them for a fiver a pop. But experience has taught me one thing for certain: no one ever pulls it off on their own.

Seriously, I've been in and around enough beleaguered bands to know a dysfunctional unit when I see one. The blend of personalities is everything and, rather like in a struggling family, people end up clashing in various ways that – when added up – make any sort of forward motion seem almost impossible. You kind of stop noticing how crap things are after a while, and begin to believe that all pop groups have something slightly hopeless and tragic about them. And then one day you meet a bunch of people like Coldplay, the sun comes out and you realise what was missing.

Anyone who's watched Coldplay play a show will tell you that, on a good night, they can be a proper, fuck-off live experience. Lots of people – even some of their fans – don't buy this beforehand, but believe me, it's the truth. Oxfam concert representative and honorary roadie-with-a-collared-shirt Chris Rose has said to us that while working at his stall in the foyer he's heard countless remarks from inbound punters such as, 'Yeah, the first album's not bad. I quite like that song, what's it called, "Trouble"?' Invariably, he'll then spot the same bunch of folks go flying past his stand the other way and out into the night two hours later, sweat-drenched and filled with rock 'n' roll glee, almost *screeching* stuff at each other like: 'Holy FUCK! Man, did those guys kick out the fuckin' JAMS or what?!'

Or, in England: 'I say, bloody hell! That was really good, wasn't it?'

As with all the best groups, this ability to hook straight into the main grid seems to spring from a deep well of collective, secret power that the members themselves sometimes struggle to trace and may not even understand completely. I love the way bands work and could bang on about this stuff for hours, but it all boils down to the fact that any of the truly great beat combo's from Elvis, Scotty Moore, Bill Black and DJ Fontana down have been amazingly lucky to encounter each other and conjure up stuff that the rest of us can only dream about. I've had some exciting moments playing rock 'n' roll over the years and even got close to the magic by joining in with my current bosses (not to mention Elastica before they wilted), but can you imagine what it feels like to be *in* a band like that? It's got to be one of the best things you can do with your mates, right?

I imagine that any successful team of people has the same, indefinable quality whether they're a Special Forces unit on deadly manoeuvres or the staff of a really friendly boozer. It's a complex thing, but it's definitely character-based and crucial to any kind of collective achievement; liking one another helps, but there's much more to it than that. Obviously a big part of the attraction for people in teams, especially young blokes, is getting the chance to show off and gain dominance, acceptance or approval, and you won't find a clearer picture of this than when Chris Martin turns to Will Champion and asks, very seriously, 'Is this song a pile of shit?'

Will Champion, eh? What a great name. It sounds like a top 1950s bodybuilder and is about as positive as two words can get without actually being 'Super' and 'man'. It's the exact opposite of 'Won't Loser' and I'm pretty sure having such a cool handle must have helped Coldplay's timekeeper become the powerful musician he is today. In the first place, lest we forget, this lad wasn't even a drummer at all but an accomplished pianist and guitar player who decided that since their originally allotted sticksman had canned the first rehearsal and gone for a pint instead, he was going to have a punt on the wrong instrument. Now, a zillion record and ticket sales later, and Will is manning a personalised, custom-built Yamaha kit like he was *born* at it. A physically strong yet truly non-violent soul who claims to have never thrown a punch in his life, Will is also a man in love with sport of all kinds and attacks every thump of a drum or swish of a cymbal with a noticeable unwillingness to concede defeat.

Interesting to reflect, then, that out of all the band members, Chris Martin has said it's Will he's really trying to look cool in front of and impress. Properly confident, virtually unstoppable and yet scathingly self-critical, Coldplay's tireless, multitasking vocalist exudes supernatural levels of drive which can propel, inspire or even scupper him at any moment. A typical recording session, say, might begin and end with him half-shouting the words 'This is fucking great, fellas!' but you can bank on some fairly hellish periods of doubt in between, which his three colleagues have become masters at navigating. Luckily for him and everyone else, Will, Jon and Guy have pretty much always had complete belief in his talents and appear to be massive fans as well as loyal partners. Chris, like his bandmates, is a really decent, loveable sort of chap who for some reason just wants to win everything – particularly on the cricket field where, to my untrained eye, he looks like a pretty bloody scary bowler.

Of course, nice as he is, you don't get to be this big a star without banging a few heads. Chris, as you might imagine, can be as tough to deal with as any of them and if someone's going to clash with Coldplay's front man first, chances are it'll be Guy Berryman. Despite the fact that these two are great mates, share a real sense of fun and carry some pretty deep mutual respect, their tolerance of one another can occasionally evaporate almost completely to reveal some fairly rugged ill feeling. Guy, like a lot of rock 'n' roll's best bassists, is a meticulous, methodical and very serious musician whose non-flash but crucial hooks manage to tug at the listener's mind every bit as much as his bandmate's piano parts or sing-a-long choruses do. Much of the time he's as quiet, kind-hearted and gentle as any man, but at the end of the day the lad's from Fife and will only put up with a certain amount of crap before he bites. It's a selective thing, but if Guy thinks someone wants dusting off a bit he'll weigh in straightaway without any fear whatsoever, as we'll see in a minute.

Bez, as he's known to a few of us, is also a naturally supportive bloke who I've often seen take on the role of staunch, unshakeable ally, but there's not much he enjoys more than bursting someone's bubble by having a kindly chuckle at their expense.

CM: 'The thing I hate about being called a geography teacher is that really, it's not *me* that's the most like one at all. It's *Guy*.'

GB: 'But look, it says "Paris" on your T-shirt. That's part of geography, isn't it?'

One of life's true enthusiasts, Coldplay's bass player tends to go the whole hog – and a bit extra – on whatever he decides he's going to get himself into, be it vintage musical equipment, sexy cars, training at the gym or just bidding for mad old shite on eBay.

And, like his bandmates, he hasn't much time for coming second at any of it either.

So, finally, what about Jonny? And, while we're here, how does it feel to be employed by one of the most commercially (and arguably artistically) successful lead guitarists in popular music? Well, sorry, it sounds really crap and probably entitles me to a nomination for the Bumnose Booker Prize, but my actual boss is – thank fuck – one of my all-time favourite guitar players. Anyone who's heard either the recorded or live versions of 'In My Place', 'The Scientist' or 'A Message' will already be aware – consciously or not – of his ability to add something special to an already powerful tune, but I'm going to go further than that, if you'll let me.

Over the last few years of live shows, I've stood to Jon's right and watched him grow from a shy, shadowy presence into the lean ball of kinetic fury you'll see onstage today. Offstage, I've only watched him show his teeth twice – it's a scary thing because until it happens, you feel that the world is a safe place and tend to forget he's about the height of a large wardrobe. Most days, if you didn't know Jonny, you wouldn't twig he was at all bothered about anything, largely because he regularly exudes such gentleness, good humour and calm . . . well, unless he's a bit ill and then he just gets slightly quieter. All of which makes it extra surprising when the lights go down, he hits the stage at a trot and proceeds to attack his guitar as though it's trying to kill him. From three yards away it's a bit unnerving, which is actually a good thing. I've always felt that the essence of an electrifying show lies in the performer's ability to give you the feeling that, should you foolishly decide to walk onstage during a song and tell them their wife was on the phone or how Spurs had got on that night, they would destroy you there and then without missing so much as a minim.

Pete Townshend is a great example of this, having laid waste to many a hapless Who stage setup in his youth, simply as a result of being wired by the tunes and at the mercy of the audience before him. A normally peaceful man by all accounts, Pete has said that he's come close to wiping out innocent people with his guitar just because they walked into his zone without good reason. Along the same lines, if you care to trawl through a copy of the Stones documentary '25x5' there's some lovely old footage of Keith Richards nearly taking a stray punter's head off with his Fender Telecaster, accompanied by the guitarist's own characteristically lazy-yet-menacing voiceover: 'You don't come up there while I'm trying to do my gig. I mean, the guy might be a fan, he might be a nutter. Whatever, the cat's on my turf. I'm gonna chop the mother down.'

While I can hardly bear to imagine the sight of Jonny getting rigged enough to do, or say, such a thing, the truth is you never really know what's up ahead. If push came to shove, or anyone onstage was in danger, I really wouldn't put anything past him at all.

We've always got on well, Jonny and me. We find similar things funny, and share a common love of young guitarists such as Mick Taylor (Keef's sidekick between 1969 and 1974, which many consider to be the Stones' finest time) and Bernard Sumner of the impossibly perfect Warsaw, Joy Division and, later, New Order.

Quite often our downtime in the studio or on the road will be spent meticulously learning ancient TV sports themes (BBC1's pub-rock snooker intro and the all-but-the-kitchen-sink *Grandstand* opener being particular favourites), while decoding the bizarre structures of certain Pixies tunes remains an ongoing challenge to this day. It's a cool thing to do and I'd like to think that some of what we both love about music has rubbed off on one another as a result. We really care what the other one thinks too – I love getting things right for him and am fairly certain I occasionally catch my employer and pal turning his instrument slightly towards me during a hot bit of a gig as if to say, 'Here you go, you fuckin' old-timer. Check this out!'

It's all a bit of a result and I think we both feel quite lucky to have found each other. I remember one summer's morning, during *Parachutes*' early ascendance, as we sat gazing at the still, silvery waters of a Scandinavian harbour . . . no, wait, it's not like it sounds! We'd been up all night on the Viking grog after a festival and, since the Nordic world hadn't bothered to get dark, there we were, still wide awake and drinking. The last conversation we had before tottering feebly hotel-ward went as follows:

'So, Jon. You've never been a rock star before, have you?'

'No.'

'Well, that's cool. 'Cos I've never been a rock-star roadie either.'

'Right!'

'I mean, man, whaddya say we stick together and, like, grow into it?'

'OK. Good idea!'

'Sweet. It's a deal.'

And, to be honest, since that balmy, boozed-up morning, we've never really looked back.

Jonny, like the others, and in stark contrast to his nonchalant aura, also much prefers to win things than not.

So much for the individual analysis. Let's put these not-so-wee scamps together on a tense rock 'n' roll day, stand back and watch what happens.

Bimbo's – a small club in San Francisco – was the scene of a telling drama, not long before the American release of *A Rush of Blood to the Head*. A bible-sized rainstorm had made us all feel quite lucky to be indoors, as though we were in school on a wet lunch break. It was around 4 p.m. and Coldplay – who, with a combined height of more than 24 feet, aren't anybody's bunch of short-arses – were crammed onto a tiny stage, sound-checking for what's known in the US music world as a 'buzz gig', which for any normal folks still with us is a sexy name for a nerve-shredding night's work with no room to move, plugged into the wrong electricity.

The audience at a small, sticky event like this is as likely to contain Drew Barrymore as a teenage competition winner and it's usually broadcast live on local radio – which in West Coast America can mean there's a hell of a lot of people listening. Add this to the knowledge that later on there'll be at least eight or nine people in the room who could probably end a band's stateside career with a single phone call and you'll start to get an idea of the kind of pressure Coldplay were under. OK, so it wasn't going to kill anybody but nerves always get rattled at these affairs simply because no one wants them to be rubbish, and this early in a tour everyone's wondering whether it's all going to work out fine or crash, burn and fall to pieces.

So anyway, the soundcheck was ticking along all right until Chris suggested having a stab at 'A Whisper', an epic, sweeping kind of a song from the (then) new record. Although the tune was perhaps better suited to the echoey environs of a packed hockey arena than a small empty disco, the lads gamely dove in, making a pretty good start. But after about half a minute, the singer gave in and threw up his hands.

'All right, stop. Stop! It sounds fucking shit.'

A few nasty clunks followed as the song drifted up a verge towards the hay bales and old tyres, finally jerking to a halt. Then silence.

Oh dear.

'You idiot,' exclaimed Guy, mildly insulted and somewhat peeved at the interruption. He rounded on his mate and glared hard.

'Of course it sounds shit,' he spat, with the measured disdain some Scots seem to be able to save for the English. 'We haven't played it since we recorded it, have we, for fuck's sake!'

Whether it was pre-gig nerves, or the fact that he felt suddenly foolish because he knew Guy had a point, I'm not sure. Either way, Chris then temporarily lost touch with his niceness and called his friend 'a cunt' in so venomous a fashion that our loveable Caledonian felt moved to respond thus:

'I'm going to fucking hit you in a minute.'

'Well, go on then!' came the retort, sounding more like an order than an invite.

Bloody hell, here we go, I thought.

Guy has confessed to me since that at this point he became so furious that anything could have happened, and he really wasn't much more than a kilt's width from braining Chris with his vintage Fender. Instead, distracted by the sound of Will joining in on Guy's side from behind the drums, our chums plumped for a small chunk of pre-fight chat, during which Chris repeatedly invited Guy to attack him. The bassist was having none of it, and appeared now to be slightly amused by Chris's fury:

CM: (Really angry): 'Hit me then, Guy! Come on!'

GB: (Smiling a bit): 'No!'

A cussed, three-way power struggle continued for some minutes, during which we all hid behind the curtains and wondered whether anyone would have to bring on the bucket of cold water. But in the end, of course, everybody handed in their handbags and Will jumped over his drums to join the other two, pulling them into a disarming and apologetic group hug.

Jonny Buckland, true to form, had remained silent and passive throughout but soon gave us all the chance to chuckle by sighing loudly at the perfect moment and enquiring of his colleagues, 'So, are we gonna rehearse "Politik" now, you bunch of wankers?'

The thing is, little stories like that are good for a titter, but they also show you a bit about how Coldplay function as a unit. For a start, when push comes to shove they really aren't at all scared of one another, which cuts out the tiptoeing that a lot of groups might waste time doing. Plus, despite the generally held public notion that Chris is the boss, I hope you're getting a picture of a gang of lads rather than one dude and his hired help. He might be the main songwriter and the focal point of the band for many people, but – and I'm sure they'd all agree – without each other's presence Coldplay would be sailing on a choppy fucking sea without a rudder, instead of just sailing on a choppy fucking sea.

CHAPTER SEVEN

GIG DAY

'You're writin' a book, dude? Whatcha gonna say? We load in, we do the show, we load back out, we get wrecked, The Fuckin' End?'

Anon roadie, *X&Y* US tour, summer 2006

Well, he had a point. But still, there's an indignant, attention-seeking part of me that really wants normal people to know what all of us roadie toerags actually do all day. I mean, we quite often get otherwise perfectly nice hotel staff saying really annoying, well-meaning stuff to us like 'Why are you checking out now? It's only 10 a.m. and the gig's not until tonight!' Funnier still, a while back some non-roadie or other once quite innocently enquired of me as to the nature of our activities during a Coldplay show, wondering if – with blameless ignorance – for the majority of the evening we just 'hang out backstage and drink beer until it's time to go home'.

Well, no, not exactly.

The first big surprise to most civilians is usually that despite being a bit like school (go there on a bus, get teased by your mates, maybe end up in trouble in an office, etc.) a roadie's working day is mostly made up of pretty hard and sometimes bloody dangerous graft. Not dangerous like going down the mines, obviously, but nonetheless full of all kinds of pitfalls and nasty chores you might not be aware of.

First things first, then, as my nan used to say. Let's imagine it's sometime in 2008 and Coldplay are busting the world in half (again) with the *Viva La Vida* album and tour which, by its end, had shifted nearly 9 million copies and played to 2.75 million fans respectively.

If we're talking about sports arenas, in which a big portion of Coldplay's live work has taken place over the years, most are pretty much empty when we arrive apart from maybe a basketball court and loads of seats, or if it's a hockey venue there'll be a big sheet of ice under a false wooden floor as well, which might leak or have a nice, slippery metal edge for everyone in the crew to slide over on. Stadiums are a bit different – since they're three times the size of everything else you obviously need way more lights and PA to make it brighter and louder, but for us lot onstage it's largely the same deal whether we're doing Twickenham Rugby Ground or the Dog & Twat, Horley. Either way, the room plus staff, bogs, power and running water is pretty much all that's waiting for you on arrival, on top of which some kind people will, with any luck, have thoughtfully erected the main bulk of a giant, six-foot-high stage at one end.

On an average day at around 7 or 8 a.m., Coldplay's five shiny crew buses, containing about fifty sleepy/wide-awake/broken people armed with a whole range of moods and useful skills pull into the venue's backstage car park. (It might be a bit later if traffic's been an arse or the previous night's show was a daft distance away, but we'll assume this day is normal for now; as we go along though, try to picture what happens if we're late and it all has to happen in five hours instead of nine.) With any luck our dozen-plus trucks – about fifty feet long apiece, depending where we are – will have already started backing up to the loading dock and it's game on, with the vibe leaning towards that of a fish market or a building site in that it's way too early and lots of rough types will be drinking tea/coffee, pushing stuff about and shouting at each other. There's literally tons of metal rigging, extra stage, video and lighting equipment to unload immediately, not to mention all the catering and production-office stuff as well.

The first wave of foot soldiers, along with the stage manager (Kurt Wagner as we speak – our third so far) is led by a group of deceptively relaxed vertigo enthusiasts whose near implausible daily remit is to hang large chunks of our huge, heavy circus from the fucking *ceiling*. These are the riggers, whose central and crucial daily trick is to ensure that they and the locals are doing it right, i.e. safely and efficiently – not a task to be taken lightly when you consider what's going to be dangling above all the rest of our heads all day. Upwards of fifty metal motors – controlled by computers and big switches and each weighing as much as a fair-sized punter – travel up and down a mile or two of massive chains that are cleverly hooked to some tough steel gear in the roof. Er, pardon? Are you serious?

It's true, but don't panic. As you walk around the stage beneath all this heaviness it's comforting to know that although we're 'hanging' the equivalent mass of more than 50,000 bags of sugar, the system could safely suspend way, way larger amounts (which is a lot of rhubarb crumble, when you come to think about it). Throughout the early morning, the lads draw mad stuff on the floor with chalk, climb about, yell weird phrases, get dirty, play with laptops, swear, and – amazingly, from where I'm stood – up it all goes.

Also stomping about at this point will be top-notch soundman (or 'noise-boy') Tony 'Tiger' Smith, who looks a bit like a big roadie Roger Moore. It's his job to make sure everything's going to sound all right by the time the band arrive, the finer science of which might be a bit hard to fathom but the simple idea is to try and have Coldplay sounding as good in row 93 as they do in row 17 without blocking anyone's view, preferably by about teatime. Which way the speakers are going to point and how loud the bass is are, for Tony, two out of a thousand daily concerns that add up to a gruelling but rewarding day's work, and somehow he (and his core team – with help from quite a few locals) are able to get everything positioned correctly and sounding cool day after day, perhaps even leaving time for a spot of sonic '00' espionage after lunch.

Still, before that there are boxes and boxes and then *more* boxes to be humped, dragged and pushed inside, all containing really big heavy speakers, mixing desks and amplifiers to make Coldplay sound as loud and clever as possible. It's a hi-fi, all right, but hugely inflated – by the afternoon, masses of audio kit (often about seven tons in the air and two more on the deck) will be facing the seats, all powered by another ton of bloody loud amps. Too many PA technicians to mention spend long, tough hours hanging, cabling together and lining up this stuff until it's not obscuring anyone's view and, once live mixing wizard Dan Green gets a hold of it, it all sounds pretty smart wherever you're stood or sat.

Danny – who despite still being only thirty at the time of writing, has been with the band the longest – chanced upon the fledgling Coldplay as a teenager while moonlighting at London's famous mini-venue The Dublin Castle. He properly sorted them out that night by all accounts; fixing them up with bits of gear they lacked, doing the sound nicely, making them feel comfortable, etc., and something must have clicked into place, because he's still with us and is now up there among the best in the world. No one could deny this boy is a natural and has, like all FOH sound engineers, a job description that's so important it's almost silly. It's a bit like he's holding the remote that controls the bass, treble and volume of a home CD player at a party, except it's got 200 more buttons, there are 15,000 extra listeners and he's putting out 50 times the amount of noise. Along with this daunting responsibility comes the scarily complete trust of his bosses onstage who, of course, will never ever get to stand out front and hear what he's making them sound like. Sleepless night, anybody? Not for Dan – he naps for England, and I should know, having spent time as his roommate in the early, doubling-up days when it wasn't uncommon to hear him sound-checking during kips. I actually overheard him say, 'What line's the bass coming down?' one night. That's dedication for you.

Anyway, people who are really good at this sort of thing will pretty much treat the live sound like it's a fifth band member, almost as if a new record's being made every single night, to which end they're going to need a little bit of privacy and safety. These days in big gaffs, of course, the whole Coldplay mixing/lighting desk area's sealed with metal fences flanked by proper security guards, but in the smaller venues sound and lighting people are occasionally subject to heckling, beer throwing and even physical abuse from stroppy punters intent on buggering up their night for them. I've heard of engineers being none too politely offered their bus fare home, for instance, on account of the sound being 'shit' (often no one's fault, except maybe whoever decided to cram a rock venue into an acoustically sagging old tram shed/music hall/public convenience) and whole pints getting emptied into expensive mixing desks for similar reasons. No need, is there? Fuck all that for a game of roadies. I'm staying safe and sound up in the wings.

Lights go in during this morning period, too, which can also take a good while because, just like in Tony and Dan's world, the kit's really quite large, heavy and complicated. Hundreds of different lamps, miles of cable and enough trusses and control equipment to outweigh a small armoured car are carted about in maybe half a dozen big trucks and, according to our panel of lighting experts ('lampies'), collectively draw sufficient electricity once up and running to power a small Scottish fishing village. Much then depends on the quality of the local help and the shape of the venue, but ultimately it's nearly always down to the chief lampy to marshal his team and ensure that all's well, enabling the lighting designer/operator (Nick Whitehouse, Sparky Risk or Fraser Elisha, depending which year you're talking about) to work everything from a state-of-the-art FOH desk and make the concert look like it should.

Daft amounts of pre-tour planning, prep time and manual effort go into this. Lamps, lasers and projectors are put everywhere – you'll find them hanging above the band on wide black metal trusses, lining the edge of the stage and even placed right at the back of the venue, all operated for maximum effect by clever electronics or actual humans in hanging chairs pointing big spotlights at the band. It takes until lunchtime and beyond for these boys and the local hands brought in to help hoist the rig, and from then on there's nowhere the lampies couldn't illuminate if they wanted.

And then there's the confetti. On the *Viva La Vida* tour, each and every day, hundreds of thousands of three-inch-wide coloured paper butterflies (or bats on Halloween '08, as per the band's request) got loaded into huge, trumpet-like blowers high up in the trusses and all around the floor, ready to be fired onto an unsuspecting throng during the show's final minutes and then swept up by unfortunate after-show helpers well into the night. This stuff gets everywhere, from the drum riser to inside Jonny's massive pedal board, more of which later.

Also working like dogs to ensure that the visuals rule are the video crew, ably steered by Margate seafront-type Andy 'Twinkle' Bramley, and others not entirely unlike him. These are the people who, when not spinning choice cuts from the 70s at top volume or happily teasing each other and chuckling, make it worth your while to be sat at the arse-end of the venue by displaying dramatic images on large, posh screens for extra fun. On the outdoor portion of the *Viva* tour, for instance, the main 'video wall' – about eighty big crazy panels that actually moved up and down behind the band on the aforementioned chains – slotted together like huge, roadie Lego and each 60kg 'brick' was made up of tiny LED lights, which from a distance – like magic – became a really massive telly. Wherever possible – i.e. anywhere with a roof – this was augmented by a set of large hanging balloons, which had cool stuff projected onto them as well.

Much of the eye candy you'll see displayed on this kind of techno wonder during any concert is 'prepared earlier' like on *Blue Peter*, but so everyone's happy at the back it all gets cut in among live, happening-right-in-front-of-your-eyes band footage as well. This stuff is filmed in real time by an elite troop of brave dudes who, unlike the rest of us, have the balls to do things like go up to Will

Champion with nothing but a video camera for protection while he's playing drums on 'Yellow'.

Sod that – I'd feel safer holding a wet mop while stalking an angry bear.

Meanwhile, in a recently erected kitchen area somewhere nearby, people are most likely listening to The Specials' *Greatest Hits* at full blast while fiercely chopping large piles of vegetables. Heidi Varah and her cool gang of chefs will, by this time, have already unloaded their truck, set up a whole kitchen and gone shopping so that soon there'll be a full breakfast, juice and good vibes for everyone. It's really one of the joys of top-flight touring to know that a fantastic meal is just around the corner, or that you can get a nice cup of tea anytime, with a biscuit. (There's lunch later, and a three-course dinner with vegetarian options will be served up before show time as well.) Among the first folks into most venues, these amazing people put coal on our fires daily and their value on the road can't be overstated – tours of all sizes would just grind to a sad crawl without them.[4]

It's worth noting also that during this time the production team (Craig Finley and Marguerite Nguyen on *Viva La Vida*) will have set up camp in a back room somewhere near the stage. Far from being the safe haven of industry its name suggests, the Production Office – despite containing desks, computers, smelly candles, stress-balls and a photocopier – is clearly nothing less than an inner chamber of extreme professional masochism. I mean, how else could you explain the willingness of these two, and others like them, to

---

[4] Sometimes it's too costly to bring your own caterers – you have to first buy out the local firms in the US, for instance – and the difference in the crew's general energy level/wellbeing becomes immediately apparent.

occupy such a space day after day? Who would even want to try and organise almost everything from backstage passes (20,000 issued by Shari Weber during our 15-month *X&Y* jaunt alone) to where the hell all the buses are going to park, while knowing that the next daft roadie request is just moments away?

Most production people would probably agree that the ratio of acceptable to stupid queries that land in front of them each day probably averages around 5 in every 50. For instance:

'Where's the crew room?'

'Can my Auntie Mabel watch the show from on the ceiling?'

'What time is it in Ecuador?'

And so on.

I'm as guilty of this as anybody, and no wonder people in production offices everywhere sometimes lose their patience. I know I couldn't bear it, and expressed as much one afternoon to our *Twisted Logic* production manager Mark Ward as he was stuck to his chair and scowling at the laptop. 'So, you got into rock 'n' roll to avoid being trapped behind a desk, right Mark?'

The cowboy hat barely moved but the vibe was unmistakable.

'Yeah,' he replied quietly. 'That worked, didn't it?'

I decided to move away.

You can chortle all you like at Chris Wood's medieval hairdo, he won't care. The man they call Woody and his own special team of noise boys/girls will be too busy setting up at stage left to take much notice, knowing in their hearts that for them there's no room for error. For the benefit of readers who, like me, grew up thinking that Sir David Attenborough was Lord, the word 'monitor' doesn't just describe a type of fat stripy lizard, it's also the name given to an entire sound system that's exclusive to the stage area and renders any pop group audible to themselves and each other, without which they'd all be dishing up some piss-poor performances. If you want to see what I mean, one night this week just get yourself down to a local gig in some shit dive and check out the quality. You might think the band are crap musicians that can't keep time, but if you do it's probably not all their fault, since the chances are they can't hear a single thing the others are playing.

How Woody, Nick 'Mystic' Davis and the long-serving monitor crew regularly avert this kind of scenario in an arena or anywhere else is a bloody mystery to us all and an art form in itself, but trust me, it's not just down to fancy equipment and spare cash. You're either a good monitor engineer or a crap one and no amount of groovy appliances or big budgets will cover you in the raging aftermath of a squeaky, feedback-ridden show during which the singer couldn't hear their vocals above the volume of the bass guitar and no one in the band had the slightest idea when to join in.

These days, of course, as well as Woody's not inconsiderable talents, Coldplay luckily have at their disposal a bigger mixing system for monitoring than a lot of bands might get to put in at front of house, cleverly linked up with little personal earpieces and radio transmitters which all end up doing much the same as the big cheese-shaped speakers you'll see facing the band on any stage lip, but just a little less gruffly. Wedges (or 'Bensons' as they're affectionately known) are used, like the more modern 'in-ear' versions, to blow the live music back at the group as they play so that the musicians have a sonic marker, giving them something to tie in to. The real trick here is being able to balance the various instrument levels and make everyone happy onstage – a true challenge for the skilful and a total pipedream for the dozy; just imagine trying to mix the same show four different ways in four different rooms at the same time and you'll get an idea.

Celebrated noisy bastards The Who were among the pioneers of loud monitor usage, which can't really have helped their chronic hearing problems, but what alternative did they have? How else could you have heard yourself blow a harp solo with Keith Moon destroying his drums right behind you? Give the deaf old geezers a break!

Of course, the other primary function of these wedge speakers later became known – particularly in hard rock circles – as somewhere to put your foot. Who recalls what posing tit was responsible for starting this hilarious trend, but come on, it's genius at its most unnecessary. Does anyone still do it? I hope so, but either way one thing's for sure, you'd have trouble resting your Cuban-heeled boot on a moulded earpiece.

Out in punterworld – the scary bit beyond the inner doors and security barriers where if you lose your laminated all area pass you're basically a bit fucked – something else quite important is going on too. Eric 'Swaggy' Wagner and various other people he's persuaded to help him will be unloading cool souvenir stuff and sticking examples up on the rear wall of the merch stand, ready to sell by the bucket-load later for hard cash. You think this sounds easy? It's a whole big business in itself and takes courage, skill and not a little hustle-ability coupled with the capacity to cope with a whole truckful of cardboard boxes every day, in all weathers. And with the average amount spent by audience members on an arena tour standing, during *Viva*, at around six dollars a head, it's a pretty large responsibility as well. The days of cotton pimps throwing dough into bin bags and chucking them all onto the private jet may be long gone but the spirit lives on. It's a happy deal too as these days all the gear is top quality and everyone's a winner . . . all right, Swaggy, you can let go my arm now.

Sometime around nine or ten in the morning, I'll have worked out where I am. It'll either be in a bus bunk near the venue or a hotel not too far away, so getting to work is never a problem. Worth noting here is the fact that the backline crew are, by dint of being last into a gig and first out, often described by earlier-rising/later-working wags as 'The Country Club' or, rib-ticklingly, 'The Bunkline Boys', which I can only assume suggests that working directly for the musicians in the band is a bit of a doss.

Well, I suppose it's what you make it. While my job has changed a lot over the years (no more driving the van, just one band member to look after, people to push and lift things for me etc.) the essence remains the same in that my whole day is built around the dude who's paying and trusting me to get everything ready for him. Chances are I won't even see Jonny Buckland until he walks out in front of the crowd, unlike old times when the tough part was getting Coldplay to *stop* helping and leave the stage, bless 'em. These days of course they're all way too busy to get involved, what with interviews, promo, training, visits to the tanning shop etc. Anyway, for what it's worth, here's a typical big gig morning, starring your faithful correspondent:

09:30 – Wake up in clothes on tour bus. I'll have showered the night before and got into clean gear, so do shut up. Clint Eastwood did it in cowboy films and so can I.

09:35 – Clean teeth and, unlike Clint, moisturise, all right?

09:45 – Attach stuff to belt: knife, torch, phone and tour laminate for all area access. Put on large, steel-toed black boots. Cool, now I'm a roadie.

10:00 – Get off bus, blinking and scratching mainly bald head.

10:05 – Walk into venue for the first time and spend ten minutes saying good morning to everyone, checking out the place and seeing what the vibe's like. It's at this point I usually learn whether the local crew is either: (a) Mafia-linked, armed and dangerous; (b) teenage farmhands being paid in magic beans; (c) really cool, keen and efficient; or (d) just plain bloody hopeless. Either way, they've probably been awake way longer than anyone else and so if we want any results out of them at all it's usually worth being polite and slightly jolly from the off. These folks can make or break our day so it's best not to act like an arse, really.

10:15 – Find the band's onstage equipment, which with any luck will have been tipped (unloaded) and left somewhere nice and obvious. Thanks, Kurt. Check it's all there, then go and play Hunt The Catering Department by following some of the helpful, laminated arrows and signs that Tiffany Henry will have spent half an hour sticking up about the place. Without these, we'd all be in big trouble . . . actually, who am I kidding? I get lost in arenas anyway, signs or not. (Yeah, I know, arenas are fucking *round*, what's the problem?)

10:16 – Get breakfast while making fun of the truckers and

bus drivers, who will have been up all night on the road and are, therefore, fairly fatigued and at least partly bananas, making them lots of fun and totally easy pickings.

10:35 – Find an available phone, which might involve all kinds of effort. Payphones at venues are really getting scarce, and you don't want to be blowing your wages by calling home on the mobile from deepest Arkansas.

10:36 – Put feet on desk/tree stump/dustbin and dial number, hoping your loved one/child will be in a good mood and free to talk for a minute or two. This is one of the most important parts of the day, whatever time zone you're in. Maintaining relationships across oceans and continents over long periods of absence takes work, love and lots of patience, as anyone who's tried it will know. But, if you're lucky enough to be with somebody cool, it shouldn't be any harder than coming home to your sweetheart totally fed up after a shit day's work at the office. And anyway, 'Baby I can't wait to see you in Madrid' has a certain romantic ring to it that 'Would you pick up some sausages on the way home, dear?' doesn't quite match.

10:50 – Come off phone near tears. Or laughing. Or even feeling slightly cheeky. Head for production office.

10:55 – Say hello to prod people and maybe dump laundry. Avoid hovering, or writing '3 x DEODORANT FOR MATTY' on the runner's list. Make crap jokes, get teased and leave.

11:00 – Perhaps another cup of tea . . .

11:05 – Find other roadies. Check out any gossip from the previous night and return to backline equipment. Remove gold jewellery, replace with durable Casio Forester watch and black sweatband . . . on the wrist, not the head!

11:10 – Separate stuff into piles for onstage and off (often Kurt will already have done this for us, the old diamond).

11:30 – Get my guitar trunks, which are about big enough to contain a really fat live pig each, and wheel them as near to my future work zone as safety will allow. Bring production cases (two wheely chests of drawers only slightly bulkier than R2-D2 containing everything, from guitar strings to chewing gum, that I'll need to get by) and Jonny's big silly effects rack too.

11:50 – Take first of twelve guitars from cases in trunk. Stand it upright in black, fuzzy, foldaway rack.

11:51 – Sense dark shape hovering close by. Try to ignore it.

11:52 – Continue unpacking beautiful instruments with familiar, creeping feeling of tension and slight annoyance.

11:55 – Sigh quietly and accept the inevitable.

11:56 – Begin conversation with local plectrum hunter, who will have opened with a choice gambit such as 'Hey, that's a 1972 Fender, right?' or 'Are these the band's guitars?' This happens a lot more in the US than anywhere else, and nowhere have these types been more surprised and disappointed down the years to learn that Jonny, Chris and Guy use picks without

'Coldplay' written on them. It makes you feel bad, like half a roadie, to send them away with nothing every time, a bit like when someone you really feel for is begging for change and all you have on you is 5p. In the end I grew so tired of having this conversation that, after eight years of resistance, I broke down and ordered some custom *Viva La Vida* picks, which, obviously, stopped anyone asking for a souvenir of any kind for at least a month.

The beginning of the afternoon is kind of a watershed, providing all's gone well. Lampies, riggers, motion controllers, projectionists and others might start to drift off lunch-ward and it's soon time to pile the essential band equipment onto the stage. How this happens depends on a variety of factors such as platform positions and amounts of wing space, but wherever we are the aim is the same: to get everything onstage exactly as the band want it, which you'd better have a good idea about in advance since it's highly likely the bosses won't even be in the same city until much later in the day. This is called 'hubbing' and is pretty normal for Coldplay these days; they'll do, say, five shows near New York and stay in a hotel there, flying privately by jet or chopper between the gigs as necessary. Hot shots, eh?

So, there might be a ramp, there might be a forklift, it might even be a flat push from the trucks if you're out of doors, but whatever happens it's always nice to get a bit of help. This is where a good local crew can really brighten up your day – the highly organised union teams in parts of North America, for instance, are, by and large, tight and professional units but their strict adherence to the rulebook might come as a bit of a surprise to some roadie new-comers. A good example of this is the 'dark stage' rule which, between certain hours, completely forbids any use whatsoever of the performing area. In essence, it's a sensible union law brought in to avoid overwork, fatigue and accidents, but 'dark stage' enforcement can be taken to pretty silly levels. For instance, I've heard of hapless crew members incurring union wrath and even cash fines for simply returning to their workstations five minutes after the curfew to pick up their jackets.

The flipside of this iron grip reaches its apotheosis in other parts of the world (including further-flung bits of the States), where things can be a little looser to say the least. Seriously, I've seen some pretty ill-equipped venues all around the world, over the years: poor old desert-seared Abu Dhabi, for instance, was about as prepared as you might expect for a *Viva La Vida* outdoor show under the first actual thunderstorm some of the awestruck, whooping audience seemed to have seen in their entire lives. Local stagehands held out umbrellas to save Jonny's equipment from the water feature positioned neatly above it and we all prayed for a miracle. And on one of our two nights at Red Rocks Amphitheatre right up in the hills of Colorado (midway through *Rush of Blood* and, spookily, twenty years to the day since it pissed down on U2) I had to use an almost ancient-Roman system of rolled-up towels to redirect water away from our stuff, while the band walked out into the onstage deluge under one massive umbrella.

But honestly, nothing ever looked less safe than the concrete, damp grass and rusty metal excuse for an arena we were dished up with in Atlanta during the same tour. This gaff was just fucking shoddy and dangerous; tarps flapped in the breeze and big iron things seemed to stick out everywhere, making us all nervous just looking at them. And this was well before catastrophe came to visit in the shape of a big helping of really, really nasty weather.

I didn't see it coming, but Hoppy, being on the opposite side of the stage, said that the bank of cloud that rolled over the horizon minutes after we'd finished setting up seemed like something out of *The Wizard Of Oz* and was on top of us in the time it took him to think just six words which were, 'Wow, look at that over there.'

One moment all was calm and the next it was as if we'd all been teleported into the inside of a washing machine in mid-cycle. Suddenly, we were scrambling to save the equipment in conditions that really wouldn't have seemed out of place at sea. The woefully inadequate stage roof began to act as a sail, pulling the crappy towers this way and that, so riggers had to climb high into the rickety scaffolding to untie it and all the guitars, amplifiers, lights and PA gear were drenched in a trice. I was scared shitless, like everyone else, but it wasn't until I heard our then lighting boss – the aforementioned Mr Bryan Leitch, a seasoned sea-dog and no stranger to the odd squall – say quietly, without any trace of hysteria, 'This is really fucking bad. Someone's going to get killed,' that I realised the sort of trouble we were in. A few minutes of extreme panic mixed with top-class disaster response followed; we covered everything as best we could in any plastic there was to hand and hoped the expensive, precious gear would be all right, while trying to steer clear of anything big and heavy that might fall over and squash us to bits.

And then, as fast as the tempest had arrived, it was gone.

Shell-shocked but relieved, we surveyed the damage and quickly came to a collective conclusion: the gig was off, no question. It would take more hours than we had left in the day to safely dry everything, even with industrial blowers and no more rain, while the arena itself was waterlogged and hazardous in the extreme and no one could really be sure the storm wouldn't return. Jeff Dray decided to 'have a word with the promoter', who seemed distressed at the inconvenience and was clearly concerned that we were making a poor choice. Thankfully, good sense prevailed once our trusty bull terrier had put the following question to her in a firm tone: 'Listen carefully: which part of "We're Not Doing The Fucking Gig" don't you understand?'

Bless Jeff. He certainly had his moments.

During all of this, Coldplay had arrived, and while upset to learn of our earlier plight, were rightly worried that a lot of fans were going to be really disappointed by the cancellation. After a short debate, it was decided that Chris and Jonny would venture beyond the gates and explain the situation to the few hundred audience members that had arrived early, and sing a few songs too. Armed only with acoustic guitars and discreetly guarded by me, Hop and three armed cops, the lads charmed the pants off the small crowd, most of whom sang along and looked like they couldn't believe their luck. It was a happy, redemptive scene and a great example of a nasty cloud having a new silver lining put in.

Talk about unprepared venues, though. We once arrived in the lovely Italian town of Verona to find its beautiful old outdoor amphitheatre ready for anything but a rock concert – giant fake sphinxes from a recent Egyptian epic clogged the dank, dripping backstage stone walkways and, worst of all, our main stage and towers lay melting in colossal metal chunks on the hot, dusty arena deck. We all scratched our reddening pates and wondered how the concert was going to happen, but somehow, with a lot of sweat, swearing and a fine blend of grit and local swagger, the job got done and the gig went ahead.

That gig also really stands out for me as the night I earned my 'Heroes of Backline' stripes from our then largely Welsh lighting crew. This was for an adrenaline-assisted eight-foot vertical vault from pit to stage, without which Jonny would have been starting 'Clocks' without making a squeak, since the business end of his guitar cable was in my mouth. The factors that led to this mid-show state of affairs were various, but chiefly my boss and I were required, at very short notice, to be up and running on a small platform ten yards nearer the audience, which was only accessible by walking briskly down a ramp at stage-side (him) or jumping forwards into ankle-challenging blackness (me). This worked and I met him at the destination with his cable fairly easily, but was sadly quite unprepared for the chaotic scramble back afterwards. The synthesised, circular intro of the next tune was halfway over by the time I untangled myself in the shadowy pit and realised the awful truth – I had one shot at this upward jump or we'd miss the cue in front of 15,000 Italians. My heart was in my throat as I summoned all the childhood stile-jumping experience I had and, in one go, leaped upwards and made it back to Jonny and his guitar just in the nick of time.

As I scurried away into the wings the crowd's huge 'Oh! It's "Clocks"!' cheer sunk into my back and for a split second I pretended it was all absolutely meant just for me. You know when Lando makes it out of the Death Star in *Return of the Jedi* after a race against fire in the Falcon? Yeah. It was that exciting.[5]

---

[5] We use wireless, radio guitar gear now, presided over by the incomparable Stephanie 'RF Steph' Thompson. Way more practical, but not half as much fun . . . er, I mean the system, not Steph!

So anyway, back to the gig in hand. Chances are during the last few hours my trusty cohorts Hoppy, Bash, Paul and Neill will have emerged from the shadows in moods that, like my own, will largely hinge on how recently we all got to bed and in what condition. Neill, a tall, dark, narrowboat-dwelling roadie of many years' experience, came to us as a keyboard/digital/all-round-useful tech at the front end of *Viva La Vida* following stints with The White Stripes, Mika and The Futureheads, among others. Check out the worryingly convincing YouTube clip of a masked serial killer attacking Chris Martin onstage with an actual saw at Halloween – that's him, he's famous. Neill's job has turned out pretty crazy; as well as running a lot of bewildering electronic stuff he's become a sort of 'sweeper', to use football parlance, basically legging it all over the shop and filling in the gaps. Mending, building, programming, set-shifting, dressing up in weird clothes . . . it's all in a mad day's work for the lad whose arrival on the scene couldn't have been more timely. Paul – our newest and most recently sworn-in Country Club member – jumped aboard at short notice to help me out with Jonny's gig while I was recovering from a busted foot and turned out to be an unsackable asset, so the lads gave him a real job as Guy's bass tech, dressing-room axe tuner and all-round handy fucker/nice guy. Our sixth stagecrew member, Matt 'Milly' Miller, will arrive later with the band since he's also now heavily involved in photography, documentation and filming. Milly's main job in the gig is to 'press go' as he calls it, which means he's in charge of all the backing tracks and high-tech stuff that Neill's spent the afternoon getting ready for him, along with an assortment of keyboards and other sundry electronic oddities. This highly versatile, bonkers kit all gets hooked into the main sound system and spews forth selected musical noises like violins and extra keyboards, the idea being that on tunes like 'Clocks' you'll get a bit more stuff going to fill things out in a big gig space. This isn't always necessary – a good percentage of Coldplay's set is always played absolutely minus extras of any sort – but there are some moments where, for example, you might really need a bit of spare synth and then there's a choice to be made, namely:

1) Do you get someone extra to come out onto the stage and play it for you, ruining the band's natural balance and making two thirds of the crowd scratch their heads and wonder 'Who's the dumbo behind Guy/what is Rick Wakeman doing up there?', or

2) Do you cheat really badly and bung it all on a bit of tape?

Hmm. Well, let's have a little think. First of all, you'll never catch me calling people that use tapes 'cheats', unless they're pretending to play amazing lead guitar or doing anything else that might count as consciously hoodwinking the audience. I think there's a line to be drawn here between this sort of naughty Milli Vanilli behaviour (which, incidentally, is fine in a throwaway pop environment. I mean, who cares? It's hardly Elgar, is it?) and just, say, adding a few subtle string parts from the album to jolly things up a little, or getting someone – like me on past tours – to semi-secretly strum Chris's acoustic guitar parts offstage on 'Swallowed In The Sea' or whatever so he's free to play the organ and sing properly. The fact is, if a Coldplay backing track is ever going to malfunction, though it'd be a challenge for the band to keep playing and the world's scariest roadie moment, the group's real, raw sound on most tunes is that solid that a lot of folks hopefully aren't even going to consciously, er . . . *clock* it anyway.

The thing that's tricky with tapes or any other type of added sound is you've got to play along to this special 'click' in your earpiece to stop yourself drifting out of time, which can feel a bit wooden if the player's not careful. It's actually bloody difficult to get good at as well; I should know, I was once required to try and keep up on drums during 'Square One' at a soundcheck in Paris until Will arrived and it's a good thing everyone had a sense of humour. It's hard as fuck and not like cheating at all.

So where was I?

You might, around lunchtime, catch drum tech Bash gently bouncing up and down on the snare drum like it's a trampette, but don't worry, he's only stretching in the new skin he's just fitted, after which he'll spend a while tuning all the other drums up to the right pitch, a black art in itself that usually involves the use of strange instruments and more than a little roadie voodoo. It's not uncommon at the start of a tour to see him, Will, Neill *and* Danny all crowded round the drum riser – like a road gang stood over a hole – stroking their chins, tapping the kit, making soft bonging sounds and frowning intently.

Luckily for Hoppy, Chris Martin's onstage electric guitar setup is relatively basic and gets used on only a handful of numbers these days. This, however, shouldn't be taken as evidence of an easy roadie life for Hoppy; aside from the sheer volume of acoustic instruments he has to keep ready in various oddball tunings throughout the show (not to mention having stuff happening on *three* different stages, more of which later) it's fair to say that, for Hop, each concert has the potential to present a fresh, new challenge.

The thing is, despite loving guitars deeply, Coldplay's front man has an intriguing way of showing it and sometimes doesn't think twice before doing something a bit rash. Like chucking his main vintage Fender Deluxe Telecaster into a wide, grassy festival pit for starters. Or tossing his expensive acoustic to the front row, as a gift, mid-show. Poor Hoppy actually fought through the crowd like a heroic, swimming hound on just such an occasion to save his master's instrument, only to return to the stage wet and dripping to witness the same act repeated mere moments later.

The ability to take care of Chris's guitar requirements during the mad rigours of his gig is an art Hoppy has spent more than ten years honing, so respect and credit where they're due.

And I'm staying over the other side.

This brings us in a nice, neat, Virgoan sort of way to Jonny's onstage setup, i.e. My Job. Well, I could bore the arse off you about this stuff for hours, but really what we've got going on is about as simple a rig as a sonic nutcase like JB can make do with. Walking an echoey line between restraint and abandon is a big part of what Jonny's live playing is about, to achieve which in a huge arena, theatre, dive bar or anywhere else we will need daily:

6 x Vintage Fender '72 Thinline Telecasters (tuned in all sorts of ways from normal, standard tuning right through to a crazy-ass one for '42' that has each string tuned to a different 'F'). All Jon's electric guitars have names ending in 'y' – Blacky, Sunny, Browny etc.

2 x Vintage Fender Jazzmasters – Jazzy A and B (tarted up, normally tuned)

2 x Vintage Gibson Les Paul Deluxes (like Thin Lizzy, but decorated and tuned way down low à la Rammstein)

2 x Gibson SJ200 Acoustics (named, helpfully, McGoo and NuMcGoo)

1 x Fender Hot Rod 2x12 DeVille amplifier (and two spares)

1 x Marshall 100w Plexi and spare

1 x Marshall 1960BX cabinet and spare

Note: Amps don't have names. It'd be silly.

A few yards of emergency guitar lead, logic information cable and two signal 'looms' (which, if you look in the glossary, you'll discover aren't meant for weaving)

Plus there's one 4-foot by 2-foot custom-built pedal board comprising:

1 x flashing mute switch (cuts all sound except echo trails – handy for onstage tuning or guitar changes between songs)

1 x channel switch for less or more amp volume and distortion, which Jonny never uses (a bit like the turbo on a fast, sexy car that's stuck in the garage)

1 x Line 6 DL4 delay (echoey)

1 x Boss DD5 delay (echoey and backwards)

1 x Boss RV3 reverb/delay (echoey like in a small wet cave)

1 x cheap Guyatone Chorus (makes it go all Pink Floyd/Doctor Who-ey)

1 x Vintage Rat (evil, mucky distortion like Black Sabbath)

1 x Tube Screamer (sort of 80s rock overdrive)

1 x Power Screamer (new wave thrashy version of above . . . see intro of 'Politik' etc.)

1 x Boss TU2 Digital Tuner (for tuning!)

Volume Pedal and two Expression Pedals, for causing swell and messing with outboard effects during songs.

Lots of weapons-grade, high-performance foot-buttons for switching all the above stuff in and out (these are, according to Mike Hill – who built the rig for us – guaranteed up to a million stomps. Right.)

Linked to all this, off to Jonny's side in my under-stage guitar world, is a large, crazy rack like a roadie one-armed bandit full up with tons of sound processing, routing and switching kit that, allegedly, I'm in total control of. For the anoraks still reading, it contains:

Signal Distro and Switching Units, for sending everything to the right places and selecting a source (e.g. radio guitar pack or cable)

2 x Shure Dual Radio Receivers (main and spare – you can't get *The Archers* on either of these, I've tried it)

1 x global level controller, so you can up the overall volume level if one guitar's a bit shyer than the rest

2 x TC2290 delay units – great for pure, perfect-sounding echoes . . . kind of a fjord-y vibe that's super-clean and Danish

2 x Line 6 Echo Pro units – more handy for fucked-up, screwy delays that hopefully don't exist anywhere in reality and might do your head in.

2 x Eventide H7600 – an insanely overcapable piece of high-end silliness that probably contains the secret answer to the Music of the Spheres. Eno – who else? – showed us how you could get some incredible, other-worldly noises out of this device but it (and its user manual) are way too aloof so I've stuck it near the bottom of the rack, just to teach it some humility.

A full set of illuminated control buttons, just for me, so I can help Jonny out if he's too busy showing off to get to the onstage pedal board himself.

1 x Midi Controller – Basically, it's just this thing with switches on it that's really useful! Google 'MIDI' (Musically Instrument Digital Interface) if you're that arsed, but I'm not. It's basically a time-saving way of getting song and effect changes happening fast, really. Mysterious, amazing and very clever but ultimately not much of a page-turner.

That'll do, I reckon.

There's a proper spare rig now too – basically a smaller version of the above that's always plugged in, mic'd up and ready to go – along with other vital little bits of kit like plectrums/picks, capos (pitch-changing metal devices for guitar necks), e-bows (whizzy plastic hand-held tools that make the instrument go EEEEOOOO like on 'Rio' by Duran Duran) and slides (glass or metal tubes that, if worn on the finger, turn the user into a blues man/strangled tabby).

But, as Hoppy would say, it's all side salad really. What counts is the guitar, the amp, the effects and how well the player works them; this is probably as important as what's actually being played – most guitarists tend to spend a fair chunk of their time trying out different gear until their rig becomes a personal thing and part of their whole style. It's true to say that no one will sound quite as good as Jonny through his equipment – it's been gradually built up around him from nothing over ten or more years, in which time his amount of guitars, amps and toys has more than trebled – and his playing moulds itself to the noises he can make, too. A big percentage of our favourite guitarists (Jimi Hendrix is a good example of this) have been positively *limited* by their equipment and sound like they're fighting to wring heaven, hell and earth out of what's basically a bunch of wood, wires and gadgetry straining to match up to the task, as if player and played are at the mercy of one another; the sound and sight of which, on a good night, can be sweet and powerful enough to tear the breath right out of your chest.

Coldplay's stage stuff, once unpacked and up on stage, looks pretty compact and modest for a big band (excess isn't really what any of us are about) and anyway, we all agree that a small-looking backline is just cooler. It's great to set up at sheds (outdoor, semi-covered arenas with a bit of cheap, sloping lawn at the back), football stadiums, hockey venues and large festivals with the same amount of visible gear you might use for a half-empty Tuesday night support slot down the local pub. Modern PAs are so powerful that there just isn't the need for the insane onstage volume of the 1960s, although that said, from the way Roger Daltrey describes The Who's early live outings (in Dave Marsh's book *Before I Get Old: The Story of The Who*), you can't help thinking it must have all been a right old laugh:

In them days it was all psychological warfare. We hit on the idea of having the biggest cabinets you've ever seen in your life, yet inside, we'd have this little twelve-inch speaker at the bottom. People used to come and see us and say, 'Gah, they must be good, look at the size of their gear!'

Of course, this sort of thinking can lead to all manner of Spinal Tap-esque embarrassments. At the 2006 Grammy ceremony in Anaheim, CA (where, incidentally, I had a go on Bruce Springsteen's 'Born To Run' Fender Telecaster but Coldplay came away with a career-affirming zero awards), that day's winning team, U2, hit a snag as one of their rolling risers became completely stuck on the stage-side ramp. It was just too large and, in the end, took fifteen stagehands and a forklift driver half an hour to shift. Really funny – even Sammy, their drum roadie of twenty-five years plus, was laughing – and not punk rock in the slightest!

Still, at least all their backline's actually switched on, eh? Not like some daft twats who pile the stacks right up high even now, forty-five years after Townshend and Entwistle first did it, just to try and look louder (AC/DC and a few other acts are exempt from criticism here on a rock 'n' roll points basis). There's something we at Coldplay HQ like about not having 150 guitar amps and the world's most inflated drum kit on the stage; it just looks tidier under the lights for a start, not to mention being quicker and easier to pack up . . . although, if you've got the dough, anything's possible, as one big band proved at the height of their pomp by having a whole truck just for the drum kit, which, I heard, stayed set up throughout journeys on its own wheely platform.

It takes me maybe three or four hours – less if we're late, perhaps more if I'm feeling especially anal and there's time to spare – to get everything set up nicely for Jonny. There's all sorts of cabling, positioning of amps and tuning up to do, along with various radio tests and preparing spare stuff for those awful, shit-the-bed technical moments. It's a fair cop to surmise that once I start pottering I really can't bear to stop; call me an obsessive, girly twat and I'll just smile and carry on, I love it and that's that. Also I don't really do things in any set order, which makes each day different and thus mainly free from monotony. With a nice cup of tea lined up, once you get tidying and polishing it's possible to think about something else entirely and not get hassled by anyone at all for absolutely ages. Lovely.

My roadie peace and quiet normally get shattered around 2 p.m. though. Wait a minute, what *is* that? Are the carps rebuilding the stage? No, it's Bash on drums accompanied by horrible, loud, nuclear bomb noises that are being used to test the PA, followed by the same ear-twatting Annie Lennox song Tony's been playing to us for the past seven years in the hope that it might be a 'grower'. Grim stuff, but I can't complain as soon I'll be making some fairly non-pastoral racket of my own, which, if I'm honest, has become one of the real highlights of my day. I mean, if you'd come and found me in Nan's old scullery aged fourteen with my first electric guitar (Kay SG, £10) and amp (Leo five watt, £10), and told me that twenty-five years on I'd be getting the same thrill off a noisy A-major chord every afternoon, but in a massive rock-star venue for cash . . . well, I'd have probably told you to fuck off because that's what I was like then, and besides, you'd have been bothering me when I was trying to learn the intro to 'Pretty Vacant'. But still, what total fun and power.

That said, we in the Country Club do have a rule that seeks to prevent excessive musical indulgence – more than five minutes' audible 'practice' will place a roadie firmly in the metaphorical Sin Bin, in which the strictest real and/or virtual punishments are meted out such as having to fetch drinks for everybody or don arseless chaps for the show's duration. Obviously it's an effective deterrent as 'noodling' among the Coldplay crew is now at a record minimum level, though we do have time for the odd sonically offensive gang rendition of something really basic. 'Punk Viva' got pretty good for a while, but my personal favourite 'crew jam' (which, as ever, gathered itself under the floating, multipurpose pun-name of 'Oldlay') took place at a far-flung awards ceremony in Halifax,

Nova Scotia, during which Hoppy, Bash and myself had the entire local staff scratching their heads or running for the earplugs by murdering Quo's 'Caroline' in less than approximate time with the synth backing for Coldplay's 'Talk'. A glorious, awful din, and bloody hilarious to play.

Anyway, if you want the truth, you've got it:

AC/DC songs – particularly those recorded between 1976 and 1981 – have the best rhythm guitar parts, as everyone with good riffular taste knows. So, if I could become any guitar player – just for an hour – I'd choose Malcolm Young, their much less famous but arguably twice as cool sidekick guitarist (and big brother of megastar bandmate Angus, who'd doubtless agree with me), preferably during a fairly big show or band practice in about 1978. But next best is nearly always a good thing, and every day around 4 p.m. I get just that by line-checking through a massive PA with 'Highway To Hell', 'Back In Black', 'If You Want Blood' or whatever nasty piece of Satanic noise from down under tickles my fancy and, moments later, hearing Tony 'Tiger' Smith (a lifelong fan of Bon, Brian and the boys) chuckle 'Nice one Matt!' down my headphones.

Most days mid-tour, unless a new tune needs trying or there's a guest performer to rehearse with, the band will skip soundcheck completely and thus won't even see their equipment until they walk out that evening and start using it in front of an arena full of people. But every now and then they'll catch us all napping and just show up at half an hour's notice. This is most likely to happen if: (a) a new idea is wearing a hole in a band member's imagination; or (b) we're in a country where there's actually such a thing as a 'soundcheck party'. Hmm. Let's take a look at (a) first.

It's highly unlikely that any creative, travelling musician will come home, take time out, have a holiday and then start a new recording session with zero ideas. All kinds of stuff, potential hits included, will come to a group during the period between albums and there are few more convenient spots to try things out than a big stage that's already full of their own instruments. OK, so there's no substitute for the group getting away from all the distractions of a gig – alone together in a small room is probably best – but on the road this isn't always a possibility. Soundchecking can sometimes unearth a real musical gem, although things are just as likely to degenerate into a heavy metal jam/argument, depending on where we are and who's in what mood.

Soundcheck parties, as they're known, are a different thing altogether. On the surface, these can look and feel like slightly cheesy label-driven promotional devices, but never mind all that – they're also a great, gaping opportunity for the fans and the band to get really near each other. These little events remind me of the days when, around mid-afternoon, The Jam's roadies would pull kids in through the back door of a venue to watch Paul Weller, Bruce Foxton and Rick Buckler play a few tunes, just for the fun and goodwill of it all. Nowadays, chances are that the handful of youngsters involved have won some sort of radio/internet-based tombola but it's no less exciting for them than it was for us and the band always make a real effort to ensure that their little experience is unforgettable.

Chris, in particular, shines in these situations. He'll take requests, encourage the others to attempt obscure songs they've not played for years, generally have a bit of a laugh with the small crowd and even get people up on stage to sing with him. Fledgling rock stars take note: I've never seen this lad let an audience go to waste, regardless of any prior state of mind. And it makes no odds if it's twenty people, twenty thousand, or even just two.

Anyway, here we all are with the next phase of our day upon us. It's nearly teatime, so I'll probably be getting hungry in a minute . . .

18:00 – Having slid Jonny's stage gear out of the way and removed all posh vintage guitars from the immediate area, it's time for re-stringing.

Putting new strings on guitars is all right. You can sort of drift off and think about your missus/daughter/what's for supper, and the vibe in an empty venue at this point in the day may even be quite cathedral-esque. The only downside to re-stringing is that you have to stretch each string individually to prevent it slipping out of tune during the show, and there's something about the process that I find extremely annoying, but hey, it beats my time as a scaffolder (I lasted three months) and at least I'm not long-serving U2 tech Dallas Schoo, who told me on one tour he was re-stringing more than two dozen of The Edge's guitars every single show day.

Jonny and I, by comparison, go through about a twelfth of U2's daily string quota. I don't feel the need to re-string all the axes each day, partly because even at high revs his playing is so undamaging and non-corrosive that we could probably go a week of high-octane shows before any strings started to break . . . well, except for '42' where he absolutely hits the living shit out of poor 'Forty', mid-set, centre stage and on full turbo. I'll redo his main guitar – a gorgeous, heavier-than-normal black and white 1972 Fender Thinline currently painted with the *Viva* logo – before every gig, simply because he'll usually smack it to fuck on the first few numbers and then use it for about half the set beyond that. The strings on the other guitars, which might only get thrashed once or twice each a night, are cleaned daily and replaced in rotation so as to keep things fresh and bright without being really wasteful. (See how environmentally caring we are here at Coldplay plc? The stringforests are safe with us.)

19:00 – Oh bollocks, look at the time. I'll finish up, down tools and make my way to the catering department, remembering to wash my hands on the way, hopefully.

19:05 – Choose victuals from sumptuous menu (or groan and wish you were at your mum's if the local catering's cack) and select seat. This is normally a golden, sociable, happy time of day, during which everyone sticks grumpily to their own department and pulls faces at the other diners. Just kidding.

19:18 – Politely extricate self from enlivening exchange on the merits of the *Flashman* book collection with Jonny and Anthony 'Chris's dad' Martin (or dull chinwag with abandoned lighting crew relative) and head for bus. Possibly bump into the boss on his way to table tennis. Yeah, we carry a table. What's so funny?

19:23 – Enter dark, pre-show vortex of adrenaline.

19.25 – Change into plain black 'hope no one can see me onstage' roadie T-shirt.

19:26 – Brush and floss teeth. Moisturise, again.

19:30 – Clomp down bus stairs like a real hard nut and puff out chest. Walk towards guitar world.

19:33 – Arrive and realise there's nothing left to do because I've been too over efficient/anally retentive earlier in the day. Watch two minutes of support band and decide to go for a walk.

19:45 – Pass alongside the inevitable, daily Coldplay vs All-comers Ping Pong Grand Slam. How each band member fares during this open-ended, lifelong tournament may or may not have some bearing on how that evening's show is going to turn out, i.e. cheery and uplifting, punkoid and bilious, or both. (This pursuit kind of petered out by mid-*Viva*, sadly.)

20:00 – Head for crew room, if there is one. It's full of crew. And smoke. Make jokes, get made fun of and leg it.

20:05 – Enter second level of adrenal maelstrom. Come near me at this point and it's likely I'll be a bit too jovial, unnecessarily cheeky or slightly aggressive. Grrr!

20:06 – From now on, the evening becomes something of a cloudy, well-attended blur, with stress, excitement and multiple trips to the toilet often being the order. Sometimes I'll need to visit the dressing room for a quick, pre-gig natter with Jonny as well, but unless there's been a last-minute change to the show's running order (Elton's in town/it's Guy's birthday etc.) I won't bother him. There's no need, and besides we're both too scared around now to form correct sentences.

20:30 – Support band stop. Eek! It's time to go to work.

If you're ever backstage at any show, be careful not to underestimate the fiery, electrical crackles in the air during the final little run-up. There's so much tense energy flashing through a rock 'n' roll venue at this weird time of day that it feels like there's a cyclone brewing. Everywhere, from the deep sanctuary of the band's lux chambers right up to Row 97 Seat 50, people are about ready to go stark raving bonkers, so an ability to keep hold of your tiller is absolutely essential – at least if you intend making it through to midnight without running screaming for the car park. As I've said before, it isn't life or death, but try and imagine the sheer pressure and excitement levels in a situation made up of these four basic factors:

1) People, in great biblical droves, have paid good money to come – a long way in many cases – and watch the group play. Maybe it's the only time they ever will. It might be their first concert or their last, but either way they probably love the songs and can't wait to see it all happen right in front of their eyes. Things had better be at least entertaining, if not cathartic, redemptive and lots of fun to boot. No pressure on the band whatsoever, then.

2) The audience, in turn, are also completely stoked to be in a room where loads of other people just like them want to shout about how they all love the same thing. For any fan, it's both comforting and thrilling, like going to a football game where everyone supports one team and you get a goal every five minutes.

3) As we've seen, the icy hand of potential technical meltdown stalks us all. There's a lot of kit in the air and on the ground, just waiting for its big chance to go wrong,

so naturally we're all a bit nervous. No one (crew or band) wants things to break, but sometimes they just do and you'd better be ready to fix them right in front of all the above people at any moment.

4) Ever stood up in class, church or at a wedding and done a reading or given a speech? Or sang to anybody at all, either in the pub or at your local village fete? Who's called bingo? Or played sport with their friends and family watching? Most of us, if we think about it, have taken part in some kind of public performance during our lives and whatever it was, we all know the feelings that went with it, i.e. knot in the stomach, almost unbearable anxiety, superhuman sense of omnipotence mixed with indescribable fear of failure and embarrassment. You could conquer the world, or you might fall on your arse, but whatever you say or do there's no backing out. Face it, you're scared shitless and you want your teddy but, if you happen to be in a big rock 'n' roll band, chances are you fucking love it too. And may well be addicted.

So, with all of this on our minds, here comes that crucial window – the sacred little chunk of prep time before the show, like the rapids before an unavoidable waterfall. This is any crew members' vital period, during which the floor the band trust us to let them walk on is finally checked for trips and trap doors. For a touring roadie, it's the last-chance saloon and, yes, it has a name. We respect it. We fear it. It is our friend. We call it:

Changeover!

To the casual punter (and, in fairness, lots of the crowd quite rightly go for a pint/poo/pasty at this point) this is, visually at least, the entertainment nadir of the evening, unless of course the support act were really poor.

We're gorgeous, yeah, and talented, but we in the stage crew ain't Coldplay and we're all running around a semi-lit stage in black outfits, seemingly delaying everyone's enjoyment by faffing the fuck about. For thirty bloody minutes.

Please allow me to explain.

Well, for a start, we can't let the opening act leave their stuff showing. Chris wouldn't like it, and he might trip over something, so the local crew spend about five or so minutes clearing the decks, with the help of whatever folks the support band have brought with them. (I can rarely resist helping out with this – it's friendly, promotes inter-band roadie harmony and gets them out the way quicker.) The next task is to reset the stage exactly as Coldplay like it. When you've been with a band so long, this bit almost becomes second nature but it's still easier if you've remembered to mark (or 'spike') where stuff goes, with tape, chalk, sharpies and/or sticky labels. I'll drag Jon's pedal board back into position, switch it all on, tape stuff down and then pop his microphone stand into place, checking its height by making sure the mic is pointing right at my forehead. No, I'm not a short stop. He's just bloody tall, man![6]

After this it's time for us all to line-check again, which we take care of largely unheard by using radio earpieces through which Danny and Woody ask us to make noise with whatever instrument they might want to hear. This mainly gets done in a set order and is an

---

[6] Everybody thinks that three of Coldplay are average-sized and Guy's a midget. It's always a good laugh when people walk into a room and realise that, actually, it's *him* that's normal and they're all fucking giants. They looked brilliant stood next to Oasis.

essential move – sometimes the rock 'n' roll gremlins drop by in the afternoon and cause previously happy wires to snap, and you don't want to be finding out halfway through the first number, do you?

Changeover can often be a fraught time for the lampies, who – due no doubt to the sheer volume of light bulbs, computers, motors and cables at large – are often dogged by things blowing up right at the last minute. It's every roadie's nightmare: your stuff works great all day, then, ten minutes from show time and in front of half the town's music fans, something vital decides to go for a hike and suddenly it's you that's the poor fucker holding up the start of the gig while the restless crowd are giving it some nice slow-handclapping.

Once I've got Jonny's rig running happily it's time to check the radio systems are all still working properly, which involves strapping on a guitar and striding around strumming a bit, as if I'm a rock star. I'll stomp down onto the two catwalks as well, which is a laugh (though I always try to look a bit moody) and gives me the chance to mentally indulge in my Andy Taylor fantasies – especially if we're in Europe and the fans are standing, already squished to the stage-front barricade and up for a bit of a holler.

People in the front few rows love it when any one of us lot goes down onto these extra, sticky-out bits of staging, excited at the sudden thought that soon one of Coldplay/Duran Duran might also get that close to them. Plus it's a good chance for them to heckle the roadies and make cheeky remarks, most of which are harmless and fun, along the lines of 'Who are ya?' and 'Hey, Roadie! You look a lot like MOBY!' (this one has kind of disappeared of late) but now and then you'll hear something so rude and obnoxious it makes you have to bite your lip and look away.

Localised cheering nearly always ensues as Chris's piano is first

Bash. Mister Rock 'n' Roll to you.
Wembley Production rehearsals, June 08.

'Eyes down for a full house!' Neill rocks the shout mic.
Viva La Vida tour, 2009.

Nice ride, but where are we going to put all the gear?
Coldplay beat the Pemberton Festival traffic, British Columbia, July 2008.

Get to the chopper!
NYC *Today Show*, June 2008.

To think it *all* used to fit in a Ford Transit, eh?

Sometimes the guitars were so out of tune Jonny just had to laugh.

Audio Chief Tony 'Tiger' Smith, before and after a helping of Kellogs Frosties.

We're gonna need a bigger plane!

If I keep really still maybe he won't see me...

The nightly run to the aftershow bar was a fair workout in itself.
LA Forum, July 2008.

Viva!
New Jersey, 2008.

'Here he comes…'
Jonny puts himself between the singer and the axe, *Viva* tour, 2008.

Guy Berryman.
Viva tour, Izod Center, New Jersey, 2008.

spotted and also when the brave few climb up rope ladders to reach their – get this – hanging chairs, which dangle quietly above the proceedings, bolted to the trusses like big metal bats. The primary function bestowed upon this seated gang of utter maniacs is to 'do the follow-spots', i.e. literally trail each of Coldplay with a massive spotlight, while trying not to spill their mugs of tea.

Matt McGinn's Daily Bits and Bobs Time follows, during which I'll take extreme faffing to almost scientific levels. After ten years of setting big stages for Coldplay I've become so fastidious that it really is getting a bit daft, but I suppose if I was Jonny I'd rather have a person like that for a butler than someone half-arsed or sloppy. And besides, it makes me smile to fold the towels really neatly and tape his set list down at the exact same angle each day, alright?

Next thing I know, stage manager Kurt is booming, 'All good, Matty?' at me from the top of my stage-side stairs and suddenly a new type of tension kicks in. 'All good, Matty?' means 'Hey, pal, there's nowhere to run. We're on in ten. Good luck.'

Time for a wee.

There's something really great about taking this last little walk through the backstage area. All show-visible crew are black clad and ready at their posts, laughing and joking or being quietly serious. Walkie-talkie radios chatter away, adding to the urgency and giving it all a Cape Canaveral sort of vibe; a sense of the inevitable is at large now and there's an unspoken understanding between us all, while core band security, management and assistants all cluster throughout the strip-lit corridors in tense little corner gangs as I make my way past them and head bog-ward.

People really change in these final moments. Some might get grumpy, while others don't even want to look anyone in the eye. I've no idea what I'm like as I leg it back towards the stage but I'll tell you this: I'm alive, and I fucking love it. I return to my guitar post feeling like Beckham before a penalty or Arnie on a stealth mission, and if I've managed to have a slash too then I'm telling you, it just doesn't get much better.

From somewhere, the command for full house-darkness is given and immediately the delighted crowd – a bit like swallows all turning south for the first time – know instinctively what to do and proceed to scream their heads off at just the right moment. Some well-placed people might notice that there's a small, blue, torch-lit gaggle forming behind the stage, causing a bigger ripple of excitement to whistle through the venue; flashbulbs and camera-phones go off in the dark, red and blue lights blink in symmetry on Jonny's pedals, more isolated cheers go up . . . then . . .

Since I first went to gigs as a teen I've always tried to catch them right at the start. Something about a band I loved arriving onstage, in real life, and being finally, incredibly, actually *there* sent shivers into me on some deep level at that age and still blows me away a fair bit, even now I'm an old bastard who sees it happen every night. What nerve did it touch? Why was it so exciting? I give up, but in all my years of shows – as a fan or a roadie – the moment has never, ever let me down. So when I see Jonny Buckland striding, smiling, across the stage towards his propped-up guitar as the massed multitude roars hello, I really, really have to force myself to concentrate on the job, or I'll just snap back to 1981 and start pogoing. There's a breathless, bungee-jump moment just before my pal hits the first note and then, like four keen greyhounds, Coldplay are away.

What's going on at home or in the world at large shrinks to a distant hum in these mad few seconds, as the universe disappears and all I'm aware of is the scene that's right in front of me. From my hidey-hole under the stage, the entire cosmos right now equals a view of Jonny, Chris, a bit of the others and the audience beyond, accompanied by some extremely loud noise. I'm dimly aware of people to my left but really we're into the silly adrenaline and focus zone here – if you tap me on the shoulder I'll probably jump out of my skin, round on you and shout 'WHAT?!' right in your face.

My primary concern during these opening moments, apart from setting new world standards for iced Coca-Cola guzzling (sharpens up the thoughts for the early parts of a show, I find), is whether JB is all right and has all he needs. If he's not been at the soundcheck it'll be the first time he's played through his gear all day and – despite my aforementioned levels of fastidiousness – errors and glitches do occur. It doesn't pay to be too relaxed either; I once made the silly mistake of having a full massage before show time, which resulted in me being mellow enough to blithely saunter onto the stage after the opening salvo and hand Jonny a guitar with nothing plugged into it. What a knobhead! Worth doing just for the withering look and the wanker sign from the boss, mind.

After a few years of working with one musician, lots of stuff becomes subliminal, or something like it. There are various twitches and facial expressions I'll recognise too that serve me with advance notice that Jonny's in trouble – it doesn't happen often but he's been known to snap a string early on due to overexcitement, or very rarely a slight alteration of the levels in his in-ear monitors might be in order. No worries on either front, I've got enough guitars down by me to swap one out and re-string mid-song, and there's our instant 'shout mic' setup, with which we roadies can yelp at one another across our earphone mixes – unheard by the band, of course. You don't want them suddenly hearing halfway through 'Violet Hill' – 'Shit, anyone got any fuses?' or 'God, not this song again, I hate it,' etc. Arf!

There's a little sigh of relief once we get through the first couple of tunes, though most of the songs from here on in might require a new guitar each time. There could be a slightly different tuning, say, but it's just as likely that Jon's played hard enough during recent minutes (or the onstage temperature has intervened sufficiently) to necessitate a bit of a sort-out in the pitch department, so I might elect to run up the steps to him and swap the instrument out for a fresh one. Having six examples of the same model at our disposal makes life much easier but it pays not to get complacent – it's all too easy to find yourself heading confidently across the stage only to realise at the final moment that you're holding completely the wrong axe. Known in US roadie circles as a 'Brain Fart', this sort of thing can turn out to be anything from hilarious to catastrophic, but most times we get over it and think it's a giggle in the end. I mean, you could say Jonny makes enough cock-ups of his own, too. I remember one time in Melbourne, Australia, he played such a howlingly inaccurate note during the set's opening moments that he even made *himself* laugh. To be fair though, I'm not paying his wages, and they're his riffs as well, so I guess he can fuck 'em up as much as he likes!

With this in mind, I'll have spent a few minutes pre-show writing some fairly esoteric instructions on my copy of the set list, which hopefully will go some way towards averting any moments of cranial flatulence, although once you're a couple of months into a tour the running order has usually burned itself into your head and thereafter the set list is really only there in case of any sudden, mid-song Evo Stik flashbacks. There's so much to remember – effects-cue timings, guitar changes, dodging the spotlights, what might go wrong next – that you really don't have time to ponder it all and are best off just trusting in yourself to get things right, like a robot. This works fine until you make a mistake, of course; the hardest bit about fucking up even slightly is preventing yourself from following any small balls-up with a dive into a sort of flat spin/confidence meltdown, which, believe me, can make things far worse for any roadie than they were in the first place.

Gaffes and electrical illnesses aside though, things normally run along pretty smoothly for me and Jon until the midway 'B' Stage section, which on *Viva La Vida*'s arena run saw the lads take off and play a little mini gig down on the end of the stage-left catwalk, lit up with floor tiles in a *Saturday Night Fever* kind of stylee. Plenty can go wrong at this point, but best of all was the time I forgot to un-mute the guitar and JB was left holding a silent baby in front of a capacity crowd at Madison Square Garden. This being pre-shout-mic days, poor old Neill had to leg it across the whole stage to me and gently encourage me to switch the damn thing on.

I now have the words 'OI! TWAT!' written on the mute button as well, which seems to do the job. They don't call me Trigger for nothing . . . still, it's easy to trip over yourself here and there when there's so much happening. Most stage crew will tell you a similar tale but for my part it's all about juggling stuff minute to minute, so much of which is impossible (and pointless) to try and fit onto any sort of crib sheet, like:

'Better get a spare guitar re-tuned NOW, he might bust a string at the front of "The Scientist" and then what?'; or

'Count down . . . 5 . . . 4 . . . 3 . . . 2 . . . 1 . . . then GO from the top of the steps one chord before the end of "Cemeteries" . . . You'll just make it to Jonny with the fresh guitar and back downstairs in time to press midi button 3 for the start of "Sleep Chant". And don't forget to dodge the spotlights!'

Not to mention the special, concentrated mind-training required to prevent all the twinkly lit-up buttons and digital readouts going fuzzy before you and turning into the Plough/Orion/Cassiopeia just before a big, nasty cue.

If any of us were to write all this kind of crap down it'd take up a whole book of its own, which, crucial though it might be to us, would probably be well boring for everyone else and sell fewer copies than Mick Jagger's last solo album. Even crew members themselves don't much like to bang on to each other about the exact details of their showtime efforts (unless there's been a real howler), which is fair enough but also a pity as no one ends up with as much mutual job awareness as they otherwise might. Still, you can always learn something new if you dig in a little, hang out and ask around. It's fascinating to me, for instance, that with the Coldplay crew now being so huge, specialised and multipurpose there are people in, say, the technical end of the video department whose skills in their own field are beyond question but wouldn't know one end of an electric guitar from the other and – more importantly – have never even heard of The Damned, a concept as alien, amusing and disorientating to me as my lack of lens/TV monitor knowledge probably is to them.

The next big trick (following a mighty sing-along 'Viva La Vida' which redefines the concept of terrace chanting) comes in the shape of what's referred to as the 'C' Stage section, a physically testing full-band and security-team run all the way up to a tiny platform right at the back of the gig where Hoppy and others are waiting with microphones and a few pre-prepared acoustic instruments. From where I'm stood, this looks fucking terrifying for all concerned but the nearby crowd – having resigned themselves to watching the whole show on a big telly – suddenly find themselves close enough to dig Will in the ribs and the entire local scene goes completely bananas. At this point it's the security crew's task to ensure the safety of everyone in the immediate area, which shouldn't necessarily require strong-arm tactics, as our long-time head of venue security Jackie Jackson explains: 'If I see someone getting a bit overexcited, I'll get alongside them and tug downwards on their trousers, which no one ever expects! Once I've got their attention I'll say, as gently but firmly as I can, "Could you step back please?" Most times it works just fine.'

During this little interlude, the lads make like it's a local pub gig with Chris teasing the crowd, Jonny, himself and anyone else in range and, as usual, making a virtue out of every endearing musical cock-up. (This isn't Thom Yorke feeling a bit glum and letting us all pay to come in and have a listen.) The whole chunk's a good ruse all round and the cavernous venue shrinks perceptibly, also giving us lot back at the main stage plenty of dark time to change stuff and make ready for a big fat (and hopefully whomping) 'Politik', which will be up in a few minutes.

This is a great time of day, on any cool tour. There's no way the audience are going to let the band go, and believe me, if you've ever heard it for yourself you'll know there's not much to match the sheer head-busting power of an arena on its feet screaming for more. The thing is, it seems pretty loud when you're one of the crowd yourself, but the crucial difference (which knocks you out the first time and from then on never *ever* gets boring) is that, if you're on the stage, it's five times as loud because everybody's cheering in your direction. I've occasionally had difficulty during pre-encore duties in preventing myself from grinning like a fool, looking up from the guitar I'm retuning and giving it 'YEEAHHH!!! FUCKING COME OOONNN!!!' as if it's me everyone's coughed up their pocket money to shout towards. I mean, talk about thrills. Imagine being in a thunderstorm, on a beach, deafened by wind and waves and just loving it while being barely able to cope with the colossal, overwhelming might of it all and you should get the idea. My personal tour diary entry for 25 January 2006 sets the lucked-out tone perfectly:

> Last night in Vancouver the crowd was so loud onstage it felt like getting hit by a hot wind. I was so excited I actually went 'Woo hoo!' as I went back down the stairs!

I know, I know. Not many jobs make you go 'Woo hoo', do they? It's a rare treat, but not as rare as the one Coldplay get – all to themselves – as the lights dim once more and they return for their final few numbers.

There's a new fizz in the air during encores that most of us have felt as audience members, but for band crews it's doubled by the knowledge that the imminent dying away of a band's last chords means the time's come to really go to work. Neill shows up to my left midway through 'Politik', waiting for his moment to run up the steps and do a set change; most nights we're too tense to even speak but the feeling is unmistakable. A bunker, a pillar-box view of smoke and flashing light . . . I know it's daft but with the martial, marching noise engulfing you all sorts of crazy thoughts arrive, chief among these being the notion that, in another life, me and my friend might have been going over the top into a future that lasted mere moments.

Thank fuck we're not. It's only a gig.

I'll have started packing away un-needed offstage stuff as early as the second song in the show, but this is where it all really starts getting broken down – provided Jonny's not still using it, of course. These days we're all a lot more confident that Coldplay will just nail the encore, do the bows and run to the chopper – unlike the old days, when it wasn't uncommon to find Chris back at his piano for another unplanned encore even though the amps were turned off, the house lights were up and 30 per cent of the audience had already made it to the exit.

You might think, not unreasonably, that it's now time for all us roadies to head for the bar/shower/hotel/bus. Well, if we're in town for more than one show then this might be the case, but most nights it's absolutely not. For the lion's share of our crew, what has to happen next is the real killer, as all the amps, speakers, lights and rigging that went up earlier in nine hours now needs breaking down, packing up and putting onto trucks in less than three and a half. Scores of local helpers reappear onstage at this point, all wearing coded T-shirts so that each department will know who to yell for. This is where me, Hoppy, Bash, Paul and Neill have to move fast (Milly will usually have already legged it with the band) as we and our beloved superstar backline gear are suddenly surplus, out of the limelight and nothing more than a load of old crap that's sitting right in everyone else's way.

I usually do most of my own dismantling and packing – though at the time of writing I'm getting some great extra help from Paul, the riggers and the carps – maybe grabbing one or two local crew to help with the time-consuming dull parts like coiling cables. It only takes one overenthusiastic tugger to yank on the wrong thing and spoil everything though, so I'll politely send most other folks elsewhere until it's time to come back and trundle. 'Load Out' (or 'Bump Out' as our Australian chums poetically call it) is, from my end, a sweaty, cuss-ridden half-hour during which there's a real danger of nasty accidents; if you're looking to trip, fall or trap a finger, now's your chance as metal ramps, forklift trucks, heavy cases and highly charged, hurrying roadies all compete for space. Despite the mad levels of urgency all around, it's just as well not to rush things if you can really help it.

Once I've cased up everything onstage, I'll bark as pleasant a request as I can muster at someone in the right-numbered T-shirt to ensure each item finds its way to the correct truck, which will have a corresponding ID number, then it's quickly down whatever's left of my stairs to round up and put away any remaining offstage guitar-world kit. The real trick here is to have pre-plotted a route out to the trucks earlier in the day, thus avoiding any 'moat of shite' hassles which could easily delay my beeline for the loading dock; giant cables, trusses and amp-racks can appear right across your path at a moment's notice, blocking any escape as effectively as a portcullis and thwarting the whole, dual-faceted purpose of all this velocity, which is, simply: (a) to get our backline gear stacked up in the truck double-quick; and (b) to find a source of cold beer and pizza as quickly as possible.

This is where a good truck driver, who knows the order of the 'pack', can really make a difference, along with a sharp, well-versed set of local pushers and lifters. (*Viva* production manager Fin even dove in on backline truck duties himself, which was good of him.) Of course, you don't always get this. How many roadies reading this have seen precious stuff go onto the wrong vehicle? Or get completely lost? Or dropped off ramps? If you thought about it for too long, Load Out would make you more nervous than the show itself ever did.

Once done, we remove our sweaty gloves, thank the locals and get the hell out of the way. If we're in an arena or shed, there's at least another 120 minutes of hard work for Kurt and the crew ahead and the last thing they want to see is us lot hanging about on the dock with a chilled ale, smiling.

But sorry, lads. The end of a night's work can only be truly marked by one delicious, bottled, green, German source of delight. So . . .

00:00 – Mop brow. Breathe deep. It's done.

00:01 – Switch on phone, check for sexy texts from home.

00:05 – Find an empty office. Call cheeky texter if time difference allows.

00:10 – Get towels and locate poshest shower, usually in bands' recently vacated dressing room or an empty management office.

00:11 – Luxuriate in vast, oceanic sense of achievement, hot water and lather. Or curse scummy, broken venue, re-dress and go in search of facilities that include non-freezing spray. (This bit's negated if we're heading for a hotel.)

00:28 – Hit bus. Find pizza. And . . .

00:30 – It's all about the Beck's, kids. Plain, ice cold and beautifully simple.

Gradually the other lads and lasses finish their respective tasks, get cleaned up and drift wearily back towards our shiny, rolling homes. Some will sleep, some won't, but whatever happens we know there's another day waiting for us a few hours up the road. The driver makes a head count and, if all are aboard, the final call goes up, drawing a line under it all at last:

'We're a bus, guys. We're outta here.'

CHAPTER EIGHT

BUS WENDY
(IN WHICH MATT SAVES A LIFE)

In the context of a rock 'n' roll tour, the term 'Bus Wendy' or, less pleasantly, 'Bus Bitch', doesn't mean anything as sinister or demeaning as you might imagine – well, unless you really dislike the idea of grown men cleaning. I first heard these cheeky, evocative terms being used by a seasoned tour bus veteran way back as he chuckled at my naive scrubbing down of some on-board surface or another, suggesting that it might be more roadie-ish – even, perhaps, less girly – to just fall in line, hum like a damp horse and leave grim socks, mucky mugs and full ashtrays about the place.

My first fully Pledged, sorry, fledged tour bus experience occurred just before the UK release of *Parachutes*, in the days when the whole crew and the band could still fit onto one cheapo 12-berth converted double-decker. For those of you that, so far, have never managed to set foot inside one of these crazy tubs I'll tell you now, it isn't the Ritz, the Radisson or even Dame Bogey's Dismal Towers. In Europe, budget tour buses are often nothing more than busted-up old civilian wagons done up for a fiver and sent out on one last, breathless commercial burn. Bunks are on the top level, in rows either side of a central aisle, and there's a skimpy curtain to separate those kipping from the constant party going on in what's called the 'Back Lounge', which is really just a table full of badness with soft bench seats curved around it, a TV/DVD/hi-fi, a fridge and a small, overflowing bin-load of empties for evidence. Downstairs there'll be a galley kitchen and another little lounge area for the use of any grown-ups who might prefer wine, cheese and card games to shouting their way through another mountain of the hard stuff, and as for the bogs . . . well, yeah. Weeing only is the rule – you gotta get off for a number two – but still, using them can be a bit fucking icky and not very cool at all.

Although, on points, nothing like as uncool or icky as the following:

No sober, clean, half-groovy male tour bus dweller would ever admit to having played a part but, just as UFO sightings continue to keep regular folks hooked, the 'Crusty Bunksock' legend manages to linger around bus-battered roadies like a really wrong whiff. You might well ask what it's all about, but for once I can't decide whether to use innuendo or be graphic . . . what the fuck, look away now if you're easily upset.

On finding themselves road-bound and far from any sort of 'shared relief', the myth goes that rather than wait until the next town and the privacy of a hotel room, some especially pent-up blokes will, like boarding-school boys under the blankets, secretly wank/jerk off/feed the ducks in their dark curtained-off bunks and direct the results into a used, and probably very sweaty, sock. Foul, yes, but it gets worse; once discarded, said sock may or may not find its way out into the carpeted walkway by next morning and end up sat right in the path of . . . yeah, you guessed it.

A Bus Wendy.

No, it hasn't – thank the Lord – happened to me during a tidy-up. Just lucky, I guess. But I'll tell you this: I draw the line at touching other people's dirty footwear, however badly it's affecting the rock 'n' roll equilibrium.

Packed aboard such a rolling beast and bound for some remote rural festival outside Geneva, we huddled up in the beds for warmth and hoped our two knackered, scaly old drivers could cope with the cruel mileage.

I feel a bit mean for saying this. We're really lucky these days in that Coldplay's crew buses (the band plumped for a rented private jet on the *Twisted Logic* tour and haven't looked back) are, on the whole, almost like posh little members' clubs on wheels – all shiny wood surfaces, good soap and soft lighting – but this was a terrible, battle-beaten old vehicle and soon became known as 'Das Bus' after the stricken vessel in the film *Das Boot*. OK, we could have done with a few of their thick, roll-neck jumpers but I'm fairly certain our little party had a better time than the majority of history's doomed submariners. Still, disaster quite literally showed up at the door one dark night, giving me the chance (with the lightning judgement only the partly hammered can muster) to properly save someone's life.

It wasn't difficult, but I actually stopped Jeff Dray from falling backwards out of the bus onto the French Peage Freeway at about 70 miles per hour. He was drunk, of course, but it really wouldn't have been his fault if he'd died – the back door wasn't shut properly and at exactly the same moment as I clomped down the bus stairs looking for a beer, Jeff leaned against it. In that split second I clocked the tarmac rushing by and my friend's look of sudden, sober horror while the rest of the crew sat looking on, utterly wrecked behind a low table, unable to have reached the poor lad even if they'd tried.

There wasn't much time to spend pondering it all so I just snapped to, got a hold quick and pulled him back in really fast by the jacket.

'Fuck . . . er . . . thanks,' he said, quietly.

'Ah, you're all right,' I replied. 'Where's the Heineken?'

Jeff still tells this story with a little gulp from time to time when we've all had a few and it's quite bracing to think that he really could have been killed. Still, no harm done, and the rest of the journey passed unmemorably, unless you count my truck-stop discovery of a sponge-like food product that went by the smart, only-on-the-continent name of Bolocake.

Tour bus life is an odd thing. It's not everyone's idea of a good time, and probably won't appeal to your basic everyday loner, plus a few days might pass before you get your 'bus legs' and learn to move around without bashing your head or tumbling down the stairs.[7] Some people never quite get used to this, though most crew come to find the perpetual rolling motion quite soothing in time and if the tarmac's not too bumpy it might even help you get off to sleep as well. A good bus – which, let's face it, is going to be a roadie's home for at least three days out of four on a fancy tour – should feel as clean, cosy and cool as possible, an aim that most high-end tour companies attempt to realise with deft installation of ceiling mirrors, leather seating, dimmable fairy lights and nice, functioning bogs.

Yeah, I know. From Das Bus to Stringfellows. How did that happen?

---

[7] This is easier said than done, especially on crutches, as I've been forced into mastering a couple of times due to roadie injuries. Have a few drinks too and see how quick you and your sticks turn into a newborn pantomime horse!

Mind you, even the finest 80s chic won't stop a 12-berth bus filled with mostly men, roadie-boots and crap films from feeling like a rumbling experiment in human behaviour, pretty lamps or not (imagine a sort of *Big Brother* roadshow without the voting and you'll get the picture). It can get pretty lairy on one of these things unless someone makes a few rules. Our bus, which is usually number four in a fleet of anything up to six (or even eight for stadiums) and contains the backline crew along with sundry cotton pimps and noise boys, works pretty well in that we party when we want to but, after years of travelling together, most folks have learned to respect one another's space. There's no smoking allowed in the front lounge, for instance, but it's accepted that if there's a noisy shindig happening at either end that night then, within reason, it's up to you to bloody well join in or sulk. Not all buses are this socially organised, especially ones containing additions to any crew who might be either: (a) maladjusted apes who don't get out much; or (b) on frickin' holiday. You hear of some real seedy, disrespectful shit (groupie sex, general unholy mess, smoking up and down the full length of the vehicle, etc.) going ahead on a few predominantly male tour buses, even when there are unhappy girl crew members aboard, which to me smacks of selfishness and being a bit of a big baby. Not that the girls are always made of sugar and spice, but there you go.

We'll have our share of dicey social interludes, too. Love each other as we might, there's plenty of room for argy-bargy once roadie relationships get a few tours' worth of history behind them. I had a fantastic row with Hoppy at some gaff in Boulder, Colorado, once, which began as a simple admonishment on his part (I was mistreating his electrical plug) and ended in near-violence and a half-hour strop (we were knackered up a mountain and there was hardly any nice air). Choice quotes from the brief exchange spring to mind, such as:

'Don't call me a cunt, you cunt!'

And . . .

'Fuck off; you're a fucking cunt yourself!'

Of course, we made up pretty quick like people on the road often do, but watch out. These grumpy-old-bastard moments can spring up out of absolutely nowhere, especially by the time everyone's deep into a long haul and a bit battered about the edges. You might suddenly see men and women who adore their jobs and wouldn't normally have any cause for complaint just erupt into bouts of moaning and bitching about stuff fairytale princesses wouldn't give a monkey's arsehole about. It's brilliant.

Once you're out in the sticks, the cramped atmosphere on board can sit uneasily with some really wide-angle views outside, jacking up the tinned sardine vibe even further. Drives between towns in the US and Europe can last fifteen hours or more, which is great if you're sat up with the driver at dawn, chatting your way through the snow-tipped mountains of Northern California, but not so good if the air conditioner conks out on a blazing day halfway across Texas. Fancy it? What would you do to stay sane? Read? Sleep? Or maybe start a travelling Cajun band?

Bored with the perpetual cycle of beer, cigs and films we found ourselves stuck in during *Twisted Logic*, Hoppy once quite brilliantly decided mid-tour to bring a banjo and a bowing-saw on board and before we knew it bus life became accompanied by a never-ending, ever-mutating hillbilly tune of dubious quality but totally pure intent. At our zenith, the 'Back Lounge Boys' could boast, as well as the above components, two ukuleles, a mandolin and some bongos (the electronic drum kit was vetoed on aesthetic and spatial grounds), which could be picked up and joined in on by anyone who happened to be popping by to say hi. Normal musical standards would insist that we were largely shite, but still, our sonic collective definitely had some crystalline moments. The frequent and drunken mob-handed renditions of our own Carter Family-inspired Hicksville homage 'I'm An Asshole, I Live Up In The Hills', for instance, will surely follow me to the grave; sadly unavailable at all good stores, the tune nevertheless remains a shining example of unbridled, inspirational, sing-along genius at work.

After a successful show with a happy, harmonious gang aboard, a tour bus can start to feel almost a bit homely, and if there's a bonus day off the following day or we're heading for a real bed, the atmosphere can verge on euphoric. (I especially look forward to fresh hotels and love sorting out the room's feng shui on arrival, like the opposite of Keith Moon really.) There's usually plenty of beer/wine/pizza aboard and nobody's mum is going to come and take them indoors, or say it's time for bed. I'm not much of an all-night partier myself, though there's no way I'd get straight to sleep after a big, exciting gig – you simply have to wind down, which can mean two drinks or twenty-two, subject to whether or not it's anyone's birthday or how much juice is left in the iPods. In fact, one of the best things you can do on a bus – particularly in America – is to climb onto your bed/bunk/shelf before everyone else, slide the drapes and get some kip, thus being up first the next morning and enjoying the novelty of having loads of bus space to yourself.

Quite often you'll find yourself seeing in the new day up front, chatting and marvelling with whoever's in the hot seat at the sight of the Rocky Mountains, Salt Lake or wherever you happen to be, as the rest of the crew snore on regardless. Or, if you're very lucky, a couple of the lads might still be awake after a barking night of complete booze-fuelled insanity, giving rise to some fine, surreal discourse and truly intergalactic use of language.

'You don't fuckin' understand, man. I said he's a (belch) TWAT.'

'What? Fuck off. Don't be a pillock! And fuckin' pass me (hic) the Jack, ya wanker.'

And so on.

These conversations can either last until lunch-stop, all the way to the hotel or the moment someone passes out, whichever's the sooner.

Occasionally there are some hairy interludes. I've never yet – touch wood – been involved in a full-on bus smash but they do happen and can be really nasty, particularly for anyone asleep in a higher level bunk as they have further to fall. Ash got hit once, resulting in a few breaks and bruises; Gloria Estefan broke her back when her vehicle was taken out by a big truck and, worst of all, Metallica lost their original bassist when an entire tour bus fell on him after he'd been flung out of his bunk and straight through a window. On American single-decker buses, the beds – sealed off from the front and back lounges by proper doors, either with handles or an electric slidy thing – can stack three high on either side of the central aisle, which makes a good five or six feet until you hit the carpet, easily enough of a drop to do yourself some damage, crash or no crash. One slightly chilling rule of the road is that you have to sleep with your feet facing forward because it's better to snap your ankles than break your neck if there's a sudden stop . . . hmmm, comforting. So your life, from the second you get aboard to the tour's last few yards, is largely in the hands of your driver, and it helps you sleep to know that he/she is a professional, sober, safety-conscious type, which most thankfully are, but some definitely aren't.

The good ones tend to treat the bus as though it's everyone's home – they'll drive thoughtfully and even muck in with the cleaning (sorry, Wendy-ing) but sadly there are some idiots out there who'll do neither and drive so hungover or exhausted that they'll have to stop for a little sleep midway, causing everyone to wake up somewhere wrong and be three hours late for the load-in, or worse.

A big part of any decent tour bus driver's remit is the successful negotiation of border crossings, which during massive rock tours can be interesting experiences, particularly on the way into eastern Ontario from the States. Customs officials are as human as anyone else – get them on a good day and you'll be through in ten minutes, with jokes, such as, 'Hey, you guys look like you could use a good night's sleep,' or, 'Y'all from Scotlaaaand?'

But on a bad night you'll need to prepare yourself for some of the least fun times of your adult life. One time during *Rush of Blood*'s raid on the hearts and piggy-banks of North America the cops, or whatever they were, threw everybody off to search the bus at 4 a.m. but failed to spot lil' ol' me slumbering happily away on their first pass. I didn't know what the hell to think upon being roughly awakened minutes later by two angry men with dogs and big torches, except perhaps 'Eh?' or 'Help!' I was told to move it out, and rather quickly. Having got dressed while attempting a little futile small talk, I was swiftly and rudely reunited with my colleagues inside the customs building where part of the reason for our rather unpleasant treatment soon became apparent. One of our number, having doubtless imbibed enough hard liquor to see a Mountie through the winter, had been goose-stepping around the customs waiting room a little earlier in some ill-conceived and ideologically stale display of objection to authority.

Needless to say we were detained for as long as possible while the bus interior was systematically pulled apart. Nothing was found, of course, but in all honesty the officials could have saved themselves a lot of hunting by just checking out the condition of some of our party. In fact, it's small wonder we managed to get off the bus at all, since my last memory before retiring was of three or four full-grown Americans trying to remove a very large colleague from the gangway, which he'd succeeded in completely blocking with his hopelessly wasted, vodka-and-orange-sodden bulk.

And then there are the stowaways. Who knows how these people manage it, but they do; as recently as right near the end of *Viva La Vida* the video crew's bus pulled into Calais customs sporting what sounded like a broken engine or flat tyre, which on closer inspection turned out to be an Afghan refugee who'd somehow managed to squeeze himself into one of the luggage bays and was banging on the door to be let out. Going back a bit further, during the 2003 tour we were halfway across Iowa in the dead of night, hours after leaving a gig, when an odd-looking girl no one recognised appeared from a vacant bunk and said in a mad, trembly little voice, 'Oh, I must have fallen asleep,' then ran and locked herself in the bog.

Now, some people might not have worried and just carried on having a few more beers, perhaps even persuading the clearly confused kid to join in the relaxed back lounge proceedings. But – sorry – anyone even half sober could have seen this chick was a bit nuts, and, believe me, having a bonkers young female fan aboard an itinerant tour bus is not a good idea. In America there are laws against carrying young people across certain state lines, especially when it's supposedly against their will, and if a teenager is crazy enough to decide to travel with a dozen unknown roadies then they might be prepared to say almost anything to the police afterwards about what happened on board.

I have to praise the quick thinking and decisive actions of our Georgian sound technician Bryan 'I toured with the Skynyrd' Kiger for averting a scandal on this occasion. Despite being in an advanced state of haziness, our self-confessed redneck chum sharpened himself enough to persuade supercool, Stetson-sporting bus driver Slim that he really ought to radio ahead for a state trooper. A few calls and a mile or two later we delivered the babbling girl safely into the hands of the authorities at a truck stop, pre-state line, without incident.

Phew! Close one. Good excuse for a tidy up, though.

Anyone fancy a cup of tea?

CHAPTER NINE

LOST HIGHWAY:
THE JOY AND PAIN OF THE ROAD

Texan Roadie: 'Wait a second boy, you ain't goin' outta the
    venue without a piece! Want me to come with ya?'
Me: 'Er, I just went out earlier and bought cigarettes . . .
    seemed OK to me. Is it dangerous, then?'
Texan Roadie: '. . .'
           Suburbia, Dallas, Texas, 2001, post soundcheck at the
                                   Bronco Bowl

Touring isn't really what you'd call travelling, as such. There are lots
of people, much braver than me, who just decide one night down
the pub that they fancy seeing Mount Everest. They'll plan it, take
time off work, get on a plane, then a bus, then a donkey, and walk
the rest (which one of my best mates actually did a while back).

Big rock 'n' roll circuses are a different thing altogether – you get
to see the world all right, but from another angle entirely. For a start,
it's not your plan. You show up on the first day and get given an
itinerary, which some invisible folks have kindly sorted for you; after
that it's heads down, strap in and be prepared to go wherever the

hell you're needed. The truth is that as ace and cool as touring can be, the schedule might easily dump you and your entourage in exciting NYC for one night only followed by two brain-destroying, beer-and-ennui-filled days off in Bumbag, Arkanowhere. Some of the most attractive and romantic places on the planet have passed us by in a haze of suburban car parks and basketball arenas, but it's easy to forget it's a job, not a holiday, and sometimes you just have to wave goodbye to St Tropez and push on to Frankfurt. Every now and then though, you'll be in one place long enough to have a bit of an experience.

I never thought I'd end up in Bangkok, for instance. Like a lot of the places I've been to with this band, it always sounded like somewhere only backpackers and Jason Bourne ever ended up. Still, end up there I did when Coldplay's celebrated *Rush of Blood* spectacular sold out two nights at the 15,000-capacity International Arena.

Apart from some scary electrical oversights on the part of the local crew (we had to send out for proper plug sockets on our first day while the lampies moved heaven and, er . . . earth to secure the previously lethal stage area) I don't recall the show itself being anything other than the usual big old blast. But, as many a better travel writer than me will doubtless have already pointed out, the city of Bangkok itself is properly extraordinary and definitely deserves a decent look. With this in mind, me and some of the other backline crew went on a little sightseeing trip on one of our days off, which turned out to be an equally awe-inspiring and distressing excursion thanks to us taking a stroll among some of the most beautiful, crazy buildings I've ever seen, before being chauffeured around a few truly poverty-torn inland waterways where people lived in shacks on stilts and shared the grimy thoroughfares with real, live, metre-long black (it might have been the dirt) lizards.

There are photos and video clips of us lot on this boat trip that really give it away. No one's smiling or even saying anything much, largely because we all felt like the worst sort of tourists, i.e. choked and ashamed all at once. Just horrid. I mean, the whole time I was thinking, if I lived there and a skiff-load of well-paid, pointing white gits in stupid hats and Hawaiian shirts chugged by clutching cameras, I'd probably feel like fishing a mini-dragon out of the river and chucking it into the boat. But no, the locals were all waves and friendly smiles, which kind of made it worse. Suffice to say we all cheered up when an old lady pulled up in another small vessel which groaned under the weight of souvenirs and beers – we were swiftly fleeced and willingly shafted which, sad to say, felt pretty good.

Later, being the messed-up, overfed, inquisitive northwest-European drunks we were, me and the crew ended up in a strip joint (my first ever and so far my last too – it's true!) but I didn't stay long. I'd had enough of feeling like the world was all wrong for one day and standing in a room that stank of stale spunk watching underpaid girls/boys fire fruit/toys out of their arses in a steel cage just about finished me off.

There are cities all over the globe in which the gulf between rich and poor is always a source of upset. I doubt that many of the world's disadvantaged people can afford to get into a rock concert, but at the end of a day like this there's nothing much for it but to tell yourself – as you drift off to sleep in your clean, dry bed – that you, your fellow roadies, and above all the band, are there to spread some bloody joy so you'd better just stop sniffling and get on with it.

Easier said than done on a bad day, of course. Let's not sit on the stairs too long here but, as anyone who's been there will tell you, the road is no place to be feeling even slightly poorly, let alone low. There are different levels of this. For instance, when I get a bit worn out and fed up I usually start feeling weepy or wanting to listen to John Denver and play cards with my nan by the fire in about 1975, though this sort of thing isn't necessarily typical; others (and me at times) might show different symptoms like moaning loads, getting a bit stroppy or saying they're going home every five minutes. We're actually pretty lucky; the Coldplay entourage – due in no small measure to the type of relationships that working amid the white heat of a rock 'n' roll adventure tends to foster – really does feel like family, no matter how big our crew gets. There's usually someone nice to turn to in the darker moments but I've still had some fairly bleak, tearful times on payphones in empty Canadian sports arenas at 5 p.m. And, let's face it, if you're missing someone or there's a problem back home and the lads are soundchecking with 'The Scientist' it's not going to be too jolly, is it?

Anyone who's had a bad one away at work will tell you pretty much the same sort of tale, which could involve a sick child back home, an ongoing break-up, a sudden bereavement, or even cute stuff that breaks your heart like how a roadie pal's little toddler went looking in all Mum's cupboards 'trying to see where Daddy's gone' just after he left for a big long stretch. These tours add up to some pretty large chunks of time a long way from home, and huge bits of lives can go missing before you even notice.

God forbid anything goes down back at the ranch that you can't get there in time to deal with. Sadly though, shit happens, and plenty of us have had to quit tours in a hurry, only to rejoin everyone further down the road with some properly glum, heavy baggage in tow. I missed two months of *Twisted Logic*[8] due to a family experience too painful to remember, let alone write about. But at least I was at home on a break when it happened. There are dreaded phone calls every year, every trip. It's just terrifying; the worst thing about our job, hands down.

Of course, like any decent firm, Coldplay and the machine that surrounds them will always come to your aid in these grim moments. You'll find yourself heading home as quickly and comfortably as the corporation can swing it, probably with a bouquet waiting for you at the other end and a solid offer of 'anything you need, anytime', which really does help no end. Still, having had a few rotten/devastating days or weeks off and then flown back out to work all on your own, you might find people looking and talking a little differently – longer/shorter hair, more/less dirt, new shite in-gags etc. – which all add to the sense of alienation. Part of being able to cope with the normal three-day pre-tour heart wrench before you leave the house and head out on the road (not to mention the one after you've left) is knowing that pretty soon you're going to be ripping into it with your mates and generally rockin' all over the place. Come along solo and, believe me, it's a whole different story.

All right, I know. Any soldiers, submariners, fishermen, oil-drillers, war reporters or long-term Arctic surveyors reading this are probably scratching their butch chins by now, but it's all relative, right? Luckily for us, rather than having to deal with the horrors of combat/frostbite/claustrophobia etc., the flipside of a roadie's potentially major bum trip comes up with something lovely, restorative and completely golden. Most nights by nine o'clock, a

---

[8] Thanks to Lou Reed's guitar tech Stewart Hurwood for stepping in here.

screaming multitude of banner-waving, lighter/cellphone brandishing maniacs has arrived at the venue with the express intention of going completely mental, the fact of which never, ever fails to at least take you out of yourself for a bit, if not actively lift you up again.

On a good day this can be fantastic, obviously. One of the things I've always dug about touring is the complete inescapability of showtime – there's nowhere to run, getting off the hook's not an option and you can't just pull a sickie, either – the audience is fucking *there*, right in front of you, one way or another they've paid your wages and at this point the only thing that might stop the concert is a missing band member or perhaps an earthquake. It's an exciting thing that you might get a bit too used to over time, the unfortunate consequence of which being that a good run of gigs coming to an end can leave you feeling really, really empty. I know – it's happened to me in a small way, but some people miss the adrenaline rush of nightly shows so much that for months after a tour, 8.45 p.m. remains a time of real anxiety and bad twitching. There are folks who've actually had to get professional help with this, although the worst after-effect I've personally experienced is a sort of unpleasant 'tour-lag', which means when I come home I'm a bit of a wanker at first simply as a result of running on roadie fumes and having worked and lived with the same bunch of geezers for ages. As an example, a typical conversation between Hoppy and me during our working day might go something like:

'OI!'

'What?'

'Where's my string-winder, then, you twat?'

'Eh? How the hell should I know, dickhead?'

'Well, you bloody had it last!'

143

And so forth.

This might sound disrespectful, but it isn't. It's just a sort of minimalist, semi-humorous, blokeish approach that becomes natural after a few weeks. You'll probably find it, or something like it, everywhere from the building site to the battlefield and it's just what happens when lads are left to work among themselves, for better or worse. It's not just the men that go a bit sideways either: fatigue, adrenaline and stress can grab us all and turn anyone into a charging rhino, at any time – if you want proof, try asking a roadie, boy or girl, the wrong question on the wrong day and see what happens.

To be fair though, by the time we get off tour we're probably all about as mental as each other, and really that's one of the hardest parts – going home.

I'm not complaining. Between us we have, without doubt, a handful of the world's best jobs. But imagine it: for a year and a half something exciting/terrifying/cool happens every day, whether it's a massive show, a visit to a new country or a luxed-out (or not), possibly rather scary plane ride. Add to this the undeniable fact that for long periods you're really doing very little for yourself and it all starts to click into place. Most days, for example, I just concentrate on how best to look after Jonny, while everything I need – from food and laundry, to transport, money and a bed for the night – is kindly sorted out for me by someone else. And then, just as everyone's started feeling like this velvet-lined adrenaline trip is normal . . . BANG! The End. Time to try and be in a house, talk to normal people and go to the shops then, is it?

It's no exaggeration to say that, for a short while after a tour, no one down the pub knows what the hell you're talking about, or you them. It's like a dream where everyone's deaf and you're The Roadie

Who Fell to Earth shouting at your friends through thick glass. To illustrate this effect, at the big end of our business there's a tale told that Bono won't stay in the family house straight after a U2 run simply because he's still at the zoo and needs time to adjust to some sort of civilian normality. All right, so he's not exactly a roadie. But it sounds like a good idea. Maybe we could all check into the Clarence Hotel, Dublin, post-tour, decompress together and give ourselves and the people back home a break?

It's a funny thing though, when everything really stops. The *Rush of Blood* tour ended with a pair of sold-out nights in Mexico City, which followed two top – if tragically brief – trips to Rio and Sao Paulo. The photos taken backstage after the final, triumphant concert tell their own tale; the looks on all our faces describe pure joy and complete relief, but above all a sort of roadie shellshock.

I remember being on the roof terrace of a fairly fancy hotel during one of these nights and hearing various members of the touring party loudly and happily anticipating 'getting back to reality' and 'having some time off with the wife'. As I recall, Jonny and I just looked at one another, and immediately knew what the other was thinking: we just felt like keeping going and would have been happy to carry right on and crack Siberia all on our own.

All right, so there's the end of tour party, the possibly plush, maybe even fun flight home, the giant sense of achievement and all that stuff which is, believe me, a wonderful way to finish off any sort of job. But there's no feeling quite like the weird, spacey one you get at Heathrow baggage reclaim for the final time, when suddenly everyone you've become so close to (or can't stand) says goodbye and just scatters. It's like when the lights come on at the party's end and it's time to go home.

I'll never forget the words of one thoroughly toured veteran who once said to me with a hug near the groaning carousel, 'Good luck, mate. See you again. And by the way, just make sure you've got something else. This ain't your whole life, or your everything. It's just a job, all right?'

You see, all the glitter and champagne-class flying in the world can't stop things going really, really badly wrong when some crew folks get home. Plenty of nicely tuned boring-old-fart types do well out of the road and get real houses, spouses, cars, babies, a life . . . I'm one of them, I suppose, but only just. I can easily recall the terrifying moment some years back when, living alone in a damp, rented basement flat and off tour for the first time after a long stretch, I realised that I'd worked my way round the world three times in a year on good wages only to come back with, give or take a tenner, the same amount of bloody dough I'd left rehearsals with. Yep, next to fuck all.

Where the hell does it all go? Well, nowadays, a big chunk of the cash gets spent on buggies, nursery fees, house and car repayments and groceries for the family back home. But, oh my God, when you're young(ish) and free, it's insane. Days off on tour are the worst, closely followed by the first few nights back on civvy street, and are perhaps best summed up by an unrelated but completely interchangeable passage from Sebastian Junger's maritime nightmare classic *The Perfect Storm*:

> A swordfisherman off a month at sea is a small typhoon of
> cash. He cannot spend it fast enough . . . the money is pushed

around the bar top like dirty playing cards, and by closing time a whole week's worth of pay may well have been spent . . . most are single kids with no better thing to do than spend a lot of dough. They're high rollers for a couple of days. Then they go back out to sea.

It's hopeless trying to recall whole, particular nights – like they say, if you can remember it, you probably weren't there. A better way would be to imagine the bent-out-of-shape drunken madness you felt on your wildest birthday, Christmas works party or graduation ball and picture yourself doing one or all of the following things with some bug-eyed, battle-torn roadies way past the end of their rope and heading back to earth like busted boomerangs:

1) Throwing yourself at a shop window, bouncing off and landing in a five-foot-deep hole full of gas pipes, breaking your leg and bruising your ribs.
2) Ending up in jail after diving into a bar brawl with off-duty policemen in a Stockholm disco.
3) Dressing up as a well-known 20th-century fascist dictator after a few sherries and walking blithely onto someone else's tour bus.
4) Strolling off a balcony when looking for the toilet and landing on top of a prostitute and her client in an alleyway.

One of the above is made up, but it doesn't really matter which. Most people have done daft stuff when they're partying but there's something about it with us lot, something more dislocated and slightly desperate that perhaps a few seafaring people might relate to.

When you're far from home for ages, it's like nothing matters after the first three drinks. And when you're off the road, the crazed roadie feelings come back after the first two. I know, I've counted, sort of.

This kind of thing is quite enough to mess with your mind on its own, without even beginning to contemplate the dire framework some poor roadie lads and lasses find themselves returning home to: angry, hurt families that don't seem to get why they're always away; the same drugs (including alcohol) that were huge fun on the bus just making them feel miserable and cranky. There might be some money left, but maybe so much has been frittered away on fast living there's not enough left to really kick back or even clear that pesky old slate at the local pub. Nowhere to live except kind-hearted people's spare rooms and sofas, no work, nor any idea when the next lot will come your way. And nothing to wear but your best shirt and trousers or old tour jeans with big, real rips in, held together with the last of the black gaffer tape.

Small wonder then that, to a greater or lesser extent, a lot of us become sort of institutionalised by touring life. I mean, to be fair, it's kind of hard not to. At the top end of the roller-coaster you might find yourself getting almost as pampered as some bands, which is a good deal more appealing than drawing the dole, I can tell you, not to mention being highly addictive in far too many bad ways. The other side of it is, if you do happen to come out of things with a few bob and a nice pad to live in, you're going to have to find a way to sustain it all, which usually means getting your arse back out there again and showing you've still got the chops. Mates become 'colleagues', musicians 'clients' and you become a 'career roadie'.

Not very rock 'n' roll, is it?

Of course, you *can* get off the ride. It's not prison, or a life on the streets, though by the time a lot of crew start to get anywhere in this business it's a bit late in the day to decide they're going to fuck it off and become, say, a schoolteacher or a nurse. Also, sadly, if you act a bit silly when you're inside the bubble, it might take you to some pretty rough places once you inevitably burst out. So things are just lovely, you're drinking fancy cocktails as the West Palm Beach current carries you off down the shore then SNAP! . . . it's a rainy afternoon in North London, you're down to that last pack of tabs and all you've got is a bit of a cold and the creeping, sinking feeling that something's really not quite right at all.

That said, some of the greatest tales often come from a place right near the edge where light meets dark, making you realise that sometimes redemption is about the same distance away as the last-chance dumpster. For instance, my good roadie buddy Neill once got oilspotted by a tour in the remote outpost of St John's, Newfoundland, with only a roll of banknotes and a bag on him. Massively limited flight options joined forces with a poor phone signal and great expanses of land and sea, leaving him with: (a) about the length of the UK to traverse in time for the next gig, and (b) one very simple but critical choice. Suddenly, no longer a legitimate, solvent stage manager but a travelling vagrant with last night's moonshine still on his breath, this lad – big, strong and useful but nonetheless hungover, unarmed and massively alone – could easily have come badly unstuck at any moment. The points at which his Roadiest Hobo tale might've turned to disaster were many and various, but here's the bit that really makes you wonder why he didn't just ring the bloody travel agent:

So, the cabby gets me to this tiny coastal fishing town after about a four-hour drive. I could've chosen to call for help from the hotel earlier but I'm still kinda drunk and have just about enough cash for the taxi and the ferry . . . I'm not actually smelling too good, either . . . fucked, basically – no phone, no cards, nothing. We round the bend and I see the boat, but . . . oh, come on, the fucking ticket office is closed! We're getting near dusk and it's misty too so maybe she won't even sail; there's no more scheduled boats that day either and I've not got the dough for a cab ride back to anywhere, let alone enough for another night in a hotel.

My man offers to drive me into town, which is like a half-minute from the docks and about the size of two quarter-mile dragstrips. I pay the dude then sit on a step and take stock as he finally pulls away. The place is empty, except for yours truly and a couple of crazy drunk lumberjack types, who are outta their minds and fuckin' fist-fighting on the sidewalk only a few yards down the kerb from me! It's like, man, I may well be in serious trouble here, y'know? Still, the mist clears, I head back to the waterfront and, miraculously, the ferry firm's back open for business. I make it onboard, hit the bar and, a very long ride later, chug into Portland harbour pretty worse for wear but mighty relieved and – get this – in plenty of time for load-in!

See, you never know when you're going to need old St Christopher to help you out, however beautifully planned and cushioned a tour might be. The truth is, however good you get at this rock 'n' roll thing and whatever difference you manage to make, it was there before you were, will probably rumble on just fine when you're gone, and is quite big and ugly enough to take care of itself, thanks.

CHAPTER TEN

GOOD MORNING ESSEX!

Touring's one thing, but once you clamber inside the radio or telly it's a whole different scene – especially with a band the size of Coldplay. Straight away, a whole new bunch of crazy variables appears, threatening to disarm roadies of all shapes and sizes in more ways than you can skin a dog. Blink and you'll miss it, look away and you'll trip over, but bear in mind that one big TV clip or radio slot might just do half the promotional spadework of twenty large gigs.

Barely visible even on detailed maps of England's sometimes aptly named 'toilet circuit', Harlow's The Square is a tiny, almost worn-away venue nestled right in the heart of England's southeastern hinterland, somewhere between London and the North Sea. As mini venues go it's a bit of an Essex cult classic so, being a pretty new addition to the pre-*Parachutes* promo effort, I was chuffed to be asked along on a Coldplay live radio gig way, way back in the pre-superstardom days of 2000 AD. Two things stick in my mind most about the night.

Firstly, there was Chris politely offering up the then relatively obscure 'Yellow' to an unsuspecting world, notably describing it as 'our new song that's actually been played on the radio'.

Secondly, his acoustic guitar on the above future megahit being rather nastily 'out', as we say. As in, out of tune. Oops.

For the great swarms of music fans who've never attended The Square, its somewhat cramped stage area doesn't really offer much in the way of workspace or escape, and if you've ever tried to tune any non-electric instrument with a live band parping away nearby then you'll know how awkward a task it can be. Bass notes boom through the acoustic guitar/banjo/lute's wooden, hollow body causing the medieval, folksy fucker to vibrate in an unmanageable manner, announcing to any roadie that it's now time to run for the quiet of the corridor.

Which I couldn't do, because I was stuck on the stage.

Still, no excuses. Not more than three years later, Coldplay and I found ourselves doing much the same type of show in Los Angeles – albeit with Lord knows how many times the amount of listeners. We were all up early one morning, bleary-eyed and on the air at Sunset Strip's House Of Blues, when calamity came to visit during the early bars of a gentle, breakfasty 'In My Place'. Pre-toast, with half the West Coast, two DJs and a 300-strong in-house crowd hanging onto the band's every note, my occasional crapness was publicly hinted at by a sudden lack of audibility in the Jonny Buckland guitar department. Oh, for fuck's sake, no. Not now! I just got up! It's too early to mend anything!

If you can be arsed, it might be worth flicking through the *Rush of Blood Tour Diary* DVD just to see my look of utter panic at this point, nicely juxtaposed with a shot of our (possibly still drunk) rock star chum as he gamely held the offending musical tool up to his vocal mic, grinning and receiving loud cheers all round. What a card, especially since it turned out to be *his* fault for twatting the guitar's volume knob and turning the bloody thing off in the first place!

Musicians, eh. What are they like?

Still, that's the kind of thing wireless jocks have always loved about Coldplay – you can pretty much count on them to show up, get amongst it and busk or chuckle their way through almost anything. As we've previously seen in the case of soundcheck parties, the band – and Chris in particular – shine so much brighter once they've got any sort of audience in, so whatever happens most public events will invariably turn into a bit of a do. Which, considering the sort of surly, negative crap some contemporary rock musicians put out in the name of *Never Mind The Bollocks*, is definitely pretty refreshing all round.

Most TV and video fun tends to hang up on similar stuff but has the added potential for visual as well as aural and technical meltdown, pre-recorded or not. Also, more crew and more kit sometimes means more likelihood of a calamity.[9] For instance, the offstage-right area of our *X&Y Live in Toronto* shoot almost became a fight club in March '06 as right before my big, mid-song 'Scientist' guitar-change the boom camera bloke seemingly lost all spatial awareness, coming close to taking both me and Jon's especially tuned brown Fender out of commission completely. As I crouched halfway up the steps ready to go, with stage manager Rik Benbow holding my guitar cable clear behind me, the operator in question – despite prior warnings – picked his moment and lowered the massive arm into a choice spot just inches above my unprotected, hairless head. A shout went up which saved me from injury but, alas, poor old

[9] *Likelihood Of A Calamity* . . . what a great emo band name.

Browny's tuning pegs and capo clattered nastily against the unyielding hunk of black metal as I quickly ducked past.

There's nowhere to run in a situation like this. Fifteen thousand people and a film crew the size of three football teams are all expecting to hear the chiming guitar outro of 'The Scientist' within the next few moments and, significantly for me, my boss is expecting to play it as well. No time to say, 'Ah, sorry, Jon, bit of an accident – got to run and get the spare Telecaster, OK?' You've just got to front it out, hand over the instrument, dash for the pre-prepared back-up guitar and hope for the best. A classic fingers-crossed interlude for any roadie, but thankfully this time all was well: the tuning pegs had held and JB came out none the wiser.

Sadly though, moments like these don't just pass, even for a dyed-in-the-wool rumble avoider like me. This deep into a tour there's just too much adrenaline, accumulated sleep deprivation and surplus testosterone at large to simply walk away and be nice. I'm not a particularly violent man, as anyone will tell you, and for all I knew the 'vidiot' responsible might well have been a seasoned pub-brawling headcase or karate expert but, dog-tired and suffering from the sort of Hulk-like symptoms that only accompany long periods of being hemmed in by stands, extra lights and lenses, I suddenly – unstoppably – found that enough really was enough. And right behind me, so did Benbow. Approaching camera world at full tilt, lunging right into the hapless chap's working space and temporarily displaying the fear-free poise of a young Eric Cantona, I volubly spat out the following:

'You CUNT! What the FUCK was that! DO THAT AGAIN and I'll SMASH your FUCKING EQUIPMENT, ALL RIGHT? PRICK!'

The poor geezer went a bit stiff, bless. He really hadn't meant it, and I ended up buying him a beer at the hotel afterwards, over a fair few more of which we ended up becoming most civil, professional and apologetic towards one another. I'd half expected some cussed blokeishness to come back to me in return, but the lad turned out to be really nice and, perhaps due to my skinhead disguise and his lack of any advance Matt McGinn research, he may even have mistaken me for someone a bit 'tasty'.

Something funny?

Anyway, at the time I might have felt a bit bad about bawling him out, but it's not often you get to holler full volume at grown men and get away with it, especially not with sober righteousness on your side and a seasoned football nutter to back you up! Obviously, I loved every cathartic, nasty, utterly male second of it.

Pre-recorded rock 'n' roll shoots are all very well, but for sheer stress and condensed grief you really want to get yourselves down to a live network television studio. In North America, where chat show colossi such as Conan O'Brien, Jay Leno and David Letterman regularly rack up audience figures equal to the population sizes of small European countries, it's worth remembering how valuable three minutes can really become, which is to say that if your band ever gets a go at appearing on one of these things while a record needs selling in the US, be prepared. The whole thing's going to be quite important to say the least, not to mention absolutely bloody hilarious.

For a start, though lots of TV people around the world are really great, some of them don't seem to get how we touring types do it, i.e. put a whole arena show up and down in a single day. This must be why they always summon us to their studio at 8 a.m., just so we can sit on our arses in a brightly lit, disused dressing room and eat grim doughnuts for two hours before doing any actual work.

On the plus side, if the local firm has its shit together, all the backline might have been loaded in for you, but don't hold your breath. Chances are you'll be shunting all your heavy flight cases into ill-proportioned lifts and along unsuitably narrow office corridors yourselves, but don't grumble because by elevenses, overwhelmed by inertia, most of you'll be close to tears and just about begging for something to do.

The run of events and general enjoyment factor at different TV programmes varies wildly, but the basic gist of a crew's working day remains the same: short of actually going back to school in an exam year most of us will be unlikely to experience a more tense, boring and galvanising episode ever again. I'm always amazed by the process of making telly; it's sort of like a high-tech kiddies' nativity dress rehearsal and on a good day can be rewarding and fun, but the down side is that for us lot there's so much hanging about to be done you just wouldn't believe it. It's the polar opposite of our gung-ho, in-and-out-again-quick, fairground/circus mentality really, though it beats the shit out of working for a living, and watching professionals like Jools Holland, Jonathan Ross and their crews up close is always intriguing, like them or not. You're looking at some serious skill and expertise right there and whatever you thought of them all before, it'll doubtless change a fair bit after a day or so of hanging around their office watching them at work.

Like any other sort of live show there's always that 'here we go' feeling and the usual adrenaline rush that accompanies having scant space for cock-ups, but with telly – even if it's a pre-record, which will necessarily be about a third less scary but equally unrelaxing – the crucial performance part's all squeezed into such a short, sharp public burst that good old-fashioned nerve becomes a sacred commodity without which you'd all be completely sunk. Screw up badly at The O_2 and 20,000 people might not even notice. But come apart even just a little on American TV and it could be time to kiss your mainstream US sales potential goodbye completely.

OK, so you either think the show must go on or you don't. Either way though, if you work in this silly business long enough, sooner or later a situation will arise that causes you to scratch your head in disbelief. Just such a moment came calling way back in December 2002, while me and the other core Coldplay crew members were hanging around drinking nasty stale coffee on a festive, pre-Christmas New York set when, with the fine blend of subservience and authority only the semi-powerful can muster, one of the top studio people broke from the swarms of headphone-wearing, clipboard-carrying young women (them again!), snuck up to us sideways and delivered the following textbook slice of showbiz insanity:

'Uh, guys, we have a praaahblem. So sorry, but we're gonna have to ask you a real special favuuur, all right? On this number, can you tell us who plays that extra synthesiser part we're all hearing?'

Well, we said, it's actually proper violins but they're on a backing tape. Why do you ask?

'Well, we're real sorry, fellas, but we gotta tell ya, last week our host wasn't too happy to find another band "cheating", as he saw it, and well . . . we need to find a way to keep him off the scent. Whaddya say someone pretends to play it on a keyboard?'

Wait a minute, we said. You want one of us old bozos to go on primetime network TV with the band and mime an instrument that isn't even on the record while Coldplay perform everything else live? Just so that your boss might mistake the swirly, chamber-quartet chords on 'In My Place' for a keyboard pad and not – God forbid – suss that it's actually some authentic, professionally conducted, pre-recorded strings he's hearing? How many rib-tickling wrongs is that in one, exactly? A crisis meeting with the band was called, options were discussed and, after much debate, a handy, presenter-placating solution was mutually agreed upon.

I had to wear a hat.

And hide behind the amps.

But there I was in full view of North America, head sticking up in the background like a roadie Humpty Dumpty, rocking the unplugged ivories with the minimal dexterity of a modern-day Satie.

OK, a one-legged hound would probably have played it better, especially since I figured that as no one was listening it'd be all right to hit any old bunch of notes, at any time. But how I wish someone had recorded what I was doing, it really would have sounded avant-garde as fuck. What a mash-up. Poor Jonny had to bite his lip and look the other way for fear of collapsing into giggles throughout, and – best of all – Mr Anchorman bought the whole con, even applauding warmly and smiling towards me at the finish!

As you can see, it's all a bit of a farce. You're supposed to be playing on a light-entertainment programme, but behind the greasepaint everyone's so serious, it's all so important and every fucker's paralysed with their own fear of upsetting the boss (who I'd hope in this case might see the funny side), but still the whole process is filled to the meniscus with such utter comic nonsense that you might as well dispense with the script altogether and turn it into a reality show.

Mid tour, with days off at a premium for rest and relaxation, some might moan and gripe about doing anything extra, especially if other departments are lucky enough to be out sightseeing, playing golf, running, shopping, getting drunk or hanging out at strip bars. Well, this balances out, since quite often we in the Country Club get to dick about all day while the riggers, sound people and visual/production crew are all slaving away doing a pre-rig at a massive stadium, so there you go. And then there are the extra little side trips. I mean, it doesn't get much cooler than landing in New Orleans on a Learjet, pulling up next to your tour bus, getting off and swapping over. This happened to us one morning at 7 a.m. as a result of some crazy scheduling which had the core crew and band doing a live TV show – Jimmy Kimmell's opening night, no less – outdoors on Hollywood Boulevard the night before a regular gig day in The Big Easy, over 1,600 miles away. No way were we going to make it in time by regular flying, so it was decided that, just this once, the Bunkline Boys and friends would get a cheeky upgrade.

The inside of the smallest type of Lear is a bit like an executive VW camper: nice, but fairly cramped and basic. There's no room for the imagined bar or boudoir, just a mini bog, a hostess, a crate of Beck's and two pilots, but nonetheless it's pretty cool; if you were all alone up there with a special pal you could have a saucy hour or two, but eight of us including two fat bastards, a scaredy-cat and a piss-head was kind of pushing it.

It all seemed so hilariously posh that once safely back aboard our rolling home we decided to celebrate with a breakfast beer and a singsong. The plane was actually smaller than the bus – it felt like we'd been riding in an airborne cigar – and none of us could remember ever feeling quite so special.

So for me, though the bonus hours are sometimes tiring and taxing, especially when TV or radio stuff gets shoehorned in on a show day, I still wouldn't miss it. I love the camaraderie of the universal crew and the band, it's like a funny fighting team amid the insanity of the entertainment world and always feels as if we're a proper little rock 'n' roll family. This sort of extracurricular vibe reached silly levels on Wednesday 18 February 2009 when, somehow, we managed to roadie a live song at the Brit Awards, at London's legendary Earl's Court, and then pull off a full double bill up the road at the Shepherd's Bush Empire with The Killers later that same night. All sorts of pre-planning went into making the day work and by the time it came around we felt like the Wild Geese without the camouflage; an earlyish start at Earls Court threw up one or two niggles, such as the stage platform size and shape being so unexpectedly restrictive that I had to shrink Jonny's amp setup by two thirds and strap his pedal board to the stage sideways (you could say it was our fault for building a guitar rig that has its own post code and town hall). Camera rehearsals came and went with the usual tensions regarding angles, stage positions and the like, which, lucky for me, threw a handy smoke screen over the fact that Jonny's main amp and speaker were actually down the road at the next venue already set up, meaning he was about to do a massive telly appearance with a rented Marshall. Ah, well, needs must and it sounded quite meaty anyway, giving that night's

'Viva' performance the handy injection of hard rock it was always begging for.

These shows are scary enough as it is; they're shot in sequence as live-as-you-like and you only really get one go at it, unless Guy's trousers fall down or something . . . actually, they'd probably leave that in. Added to this, the whole time we were all thinking, oh fuck, afterwards we have to pack up and go set up at the Empire as well! What if . . .

We needn't have worried. We'd all done so much homework that there was no way the plane was going to leave anyone on the airstrip being shot at by the local infantry.[10] Our advance team, led by Kurt, had joined forces with the Killers crew to make everything as easy for us as possible on arrival, so all we had to do was tear down the gear real quiet, sneak out of the Brits without making any loud clanging noises, and go and do our job.

This kind of crazy stuff does wonders for the camaraderie. I'll always remember the huddle of black-clad core crew in the tiny backstage corridor poring over the twists and turns in the rapidly approaching late-night set, chuckling, teasing and wondering how the hell we'd shoehorn Gary Barlow and Bono in for the super jam and whose guitar rig Killer Dave was going to plug into. Coldplay arrived from the Brits soon after in a bad mood having won fuck all and tore into the concert like they were Sham 69, which was both alarming and fabulous all at once, especially after such a long day. The show was a smash and got ace reviews in all the next day's papers. We all packed up, loaded the truck, went back to the hotel

---

[10] If you haven't seen *The Wild Geese* this won't mean anything at all, but you get the idea.

around 3 a.m. and got royally, deservedly wankered until it was morning all over again.

A major achievement for all concerned, true, but not much comes closer to sheer terror than the 2003 Grammys ceremony. Millions of copies of *A Rush of Blood to the Head* had been sold by this point, so many that everyone had stopped counting, and Coldplay suddenly found themselves nominated for the absolute apex of all accolades (apart from their kid sister liking the band, of course). The annual 'Pop Music Oscars' rolled around, and the band were invited to Madison Square Garden so they could win stuff and play 'Politik', accompanied – dauntingly enough – by the city's famous philharmonic orchestra.

Michael Kamen would conduct, Dustin Hoffman had a seat in the front row, while Paul Simon and 'Artie' – for reasons no one normal either knows or gives a monkey's chuff about – hid from one another in separate dressing rooms waiting for their moment to walk onstage and sing their human alienation classic 'The Sound Of Silence' like it was 1967 and they were still talking to each other. There were around 20,000 psyched folks inside and the whole shebang was being filmed 'as live' to later go out on TV across the entire continent, so who knew how many total viewers would be watching. That was scary enough but then we learned there was only *seven minutes* during commercials to get the *whole orchestra onstage* instead of the usual forty-five, and that amount of *seconds* to get Jonny, Will, Guy, Chris and all their equipment out of the wings and into position, while an announcer is saying to half of America, 'Ladies and Gentlemen, all the way from England . . .'

They really had to be joking, right?

They weren't, and boy did we have to Just Get On With It. I had six tough venue hands from the union doing as I asked during two half-days of rehearsal, which took some large-sized pretend bottle from me, I'll tell you. There were four people pushing the riser, one carrying the pedal board, one on the cables and little me clutching JB's favourite sunburst Fender, all trying not to trip up and knowing that once the green light's on there's no way we're allowed to fail even slightly.

If you want to feel fear in showbiz, here's where to come. If, in my working life, I'm ever screwed up tighter than I was on that night, crouching behind the timpani waiting for Jon to strike his opening chord, well, I'll let you know. All I remember is the surge of adrenaline as those familiar, slashing strokes punched in to announce we were really going to be OK, and the admiring, appreciative look I could just make out on Dustin Hoffman's face as he looked up at the band from his front-row seat.

Just the same as Steve Lamacq's back at the Harlow Square, really.

CHAPTER ELEVEN

LIVE 8 AND BEYOND

I was never a big fan of flying. I know it's safer than making a cup of tea, or whatever, and being up in the sky can be a beautiful thing. Despite feeling a fair degree of unease, some of my best travel memories are of having a window seat on a smooth night ride when the monsoon is flashing up through the clouds at a safe distance to your right, or a daytime trip when something incredible can be seen below like the Amazon River (huge brown snaky shape bending through masses of green) or the Trans-Siberian Railway (straight skinny black line on a pure white background, like the opposite of a line of coke). I've had lovely rides on twin-engine tubs like the Embraer 120 (the 'Rolls-Royce of turboprops', apparently) which at cruising altitude hums at a precise 'D' pitch so if you're listening to 'The End', 'Norwegian Wood' or anything in 'D' and you've had a few gins it can feel pretty cosmic.

But still, if you fly as much as we do, sooner or later the law of averages will dictate that it's time for a bad ride. Halfway across Colorado one afternoon, just as the dollies had dished up grub and I was chatting merrily away to our erstwhile production manager

Derek 'Judge' Fudge in the window seat of a 737, the sky beneath us seemed to disappear and the plane gave up impersonating a bird for a second and dropped like the large, heavy metal object it actually was. My stomach jumped to just south of my chin and suddenly I had airline lunch and red wine in my lap to boot.

'Sorry, folks, looks like Traffic Control lied to us. We're just passing upside of an electrical storm, hang on, strap in, we'll get you through it.'

The captain sounded cool, like he was ordering room service, but his calming words were quickly squished by a 'hilarious' intercom error that resulted in the whole planeload of us then hearing him say: 'Hey, Denver, we're looking at oncoming traffic about five miles ahead, whaddya say we hang a left?'

Ten minutes of roller-coaster action followed, minus the pretty view of the funfair. Bumping through heavy cloud like a bee in a breeze might be some people's idea of a party, but I was praying to anyone who would listen, and by the end of the flight my phobia was complete. I've since mostly got the better of it by concocting a fine blend of strong booze, hard technical data, loud punk music and a stubborn refusal to be terrified for such lengthy periods, but there's always a right bastard of an air-pocket waiting round the next cloud. I know roadies who've found themselves in the crash position while the air crew dumps fuel and relands the plane; and others who say they've even smelled burning and seen plumes of smoke in the cabin. Best of all was during *Twisted Logic* when we showed up at a private airstrip, having rushed our bollocks off to make the post-show flight, only to find all the lights out and a pair of sad-looking aviators muttering, 'Sorry, guys, broken sat-nav. Step inside the building here and get a beer.'

It was morning by the time they could fix it (by flying a spare plane in and swapping out the part) and, obviously, all of the booze in the little terminal had found its way from the fridge into us lot, with the result that Bash had – in a fine, drunken, James Hunt moment – managed to run stage manager Benbow over with a golf buggy out near the runway, knocking him on his arse and busting up his front teeth!

'OK, guys, she's all fixed, let's go!' shouted one of the pilots from the top of the plane steps, having just performed a half-minute repair job that seemed about as technical as putting in a videotape.

'Really?' I said, through a haze of booze and fear. 'What did you do, exactly?'

'Oh, just put in a new spare. It'll keep the Feds off our back and stop us hitting the mountains. Coming?'

I guess there's something about aircraft and rocky outcrops that don't quite mix. A good roadie mate of mine learned this the hard way as he held on for dear life in an equipment-laden, ex-military helicopter which suddenly started flying a little nearer the side of the deep, insurgent-lined Tajikistan valley than a normal BA passenger would feel comfy with.

'We're a bit close to the mountains,' he recalls shouting to the local pilot.

'It is better to dodging the bullets!' came the reply, which wasn't made any more comforting by the fact that it sprung from the lips of the same chap who'd been spotted earlier whacking the rotor blades with a hammer 'to keep them in line' during tricky flights.

Still, there are times you've just got to get on the plane/chopper and worry about it all in the bar later. It's part of our daily game in this business and sometimes there's nothing else for it but to sink a large gin and tonic, get a hold of yourself and fly. What else are you going to do? Stay behind? Get the train?

You couldn't do it. And certainly not on the following sort of day.

I'm not getting into the politics. Enough has been said and written by far better informed folks than me already and frankly you'd do better to listen to some other people, like maybe Bob Geldof for a start. Say what you like, this is a man who deserves respect, not least of all for basically taking a good pub nag and turning it into a collective act of global positivity. (And 'Rat Trap' is an alright tune too, when you think about it.) But Live 8 was a big fucking deal, basically – gigs like this only come along every blue moon or so and if you're ever lucky enough to be involved you won't forget it.

We were bang in the middle of the *X&Y* outdoor European summer run when the day of the Hyde Park show rolled around back in 2005. The band's early afternoon slot at Live 8 had been arranged to fit in neatly between our first and second nights at Glasgow's massive Bellahouston Park so, in theory, all we had to do was get to central London, do the gig (i.e. three songs) and get back in time for the evening performance. Yeah, easy.

A private passenger jet was booked to fly the core stage crew and essential equipment down to London immediately after the first Glasgow show. We had to pack up all the guitars, drums, amps and other cack really fast right after the gig then leg it through the departing multitudes in a blacked-out Ford minibus with an exciting, VIP, cop-on-a-motorbike escort leading the way. Any roadie – or normal person come to that – who says this isn't fun has to be a bit weird. For a start, all the fans that you're trying to get past think you're the band, which is hilarious except that they also reckon it's all right to pull faces, bang on the glass and get in the police bike's way, thus holding everything up. (You can't help but wonder how the Beatles ever got to any shows at all, never mind on time or in four pieces.) Still, after about half an hour's shouting and shoving, we finally made it to the far-flung military airbase and all sat in the van at the checkpoint wondering what the hell might happen next.

I've got a few vague, trippy memories of the next two hours but one thing's for certain: it wasn't Virgin Upper Class. I mean, Branson might be security-minded but as far as I know he doesn't tend to employ giant, scowling, fully armed squaddies as ground staff. Searches were, mercifully, merely external, and despite much diligence the lads still failed to spot my accidentally concealed roadie knife, which I could obviously have held everyone to ransom with, no problem. Having thus breached national security we were allowed to hop into chauffeur-driven, possibly camouflaged (it was dark) golf buggies and head towards the plane; a small twin-engine affair with a few single pews along one side of the cabin and doubles down the other.

I took a single behind Mark Ward, our then production manager, and tried not to worry as our weighty boxes of guitars, drums and amps were stowed in the cabin right in front of us under what might easily have been a crab net or something nicked off a kids' playground. I prayed, as usual, for a smooth ride, while focusing on Mark's cowboy hat and trying to forget my days of being bludgeoned to fuck by restless gear in the backs of bumpy old roadie vans.

Luckily the skies were on our side. As I've already explained, I'm not great with turbulence, so was relieved to land quite nicely at Luton. The equipment, and us, were then whisked off by the usual mystery driver and dumped an hour or so later at a small hotel in London's Mayfair district, not too far from Hyde Park. A brutally short four and a half hours and way too few Zs later we found ourselves backstage, blinking into an unwelcome dawn which was rising fast over the biggest international musical event since 13 July 1985.

The original Live Aid was, as people still rightly say, a true triumph of effort over chaos and anyone involved should have definitely got a little medal or something. It was a tough day's work for all concerned and frankly I'm surprised the entire sweaty staff didn't wilt in the midsummer heat – it's no wonder there were a few pops, squeaks, fluffed intros and swear words on the telly. Among many other potentially disastrous but ultimately successful features, the Wembley show was run on a newfangled three-way revolving stage, a bit like a big round cheese cut into thirds, so while one band performed, the other two hidden stages crawled with frantic roadies desperately trying to either set up or pack down in time for the next potentially life-changing spin of the wheel. Tuning into the day's events at home in rural South Devon at just two months shy of twenty I felt like I always did when watching rock 'n' roll on TV as a young musician; excited and completely absorbed but somehow anxious and bewildered. How would I ever get near the flames that warmed me from so far away? I felt as though I might as well be staring at the sun.

Musically speaking, it's fair to say that, even bearing in mind how the event was meant to be a massive, catch-all, across-the-board cash-raising job as opposed to a flawless gallery of esteemed showbiz cool, there was definitely some right old 99-carat shite on the Global Jukebox bill that day. Some of the performances – and get-ups, come to think of it – went well beyond even mid-1980s aesthetic guidelines; I remember, for instance, being made to feel fairly uncharitable by the latter-day, post-synth, past-good, well-sweaty and completely tartan-free Spandau Ballet's sickly 'We love you, you're beautiful' chat, grim proto-yuppie 'soul' tunes and garish, multicoloured, pricey-looking leather coats. You can understand my rancour. I felt betrayed, having nearly got laughed out of a party on their behalf back in '81, dressed as some sort of rural toreador. And, of course, since that night, I'd never: (a) worn dodgy outfits; (b) played bad music on guitar; or (c) talked insincere-sounding old rhubarb myself.

Mind you, the day did throw up a few vital, career-defining/reviving turns as well. Status 'The' Quo kicked it all off like only they could, setting them up nicely for their next career phase – for better or worse – and a bearded Elvis Costello busked 'All You Need Is Love' totally solo, like Billy Bragg, with sod all but a red Strat and 'do, done / sing, sung' cribbed in felt tip on his strumming hand, to the absolute delight of anyone in the world with a heart. Most notably though, Bono, who seemed to have taken the trouble to blag an hour off from his best-man duties at a musketeer pal's wedding to be there, surfed in on the crest of a cracking mullet to completely and comprehensively steal the show from pretty much everybody else. The sheer guts and taut thrills of U2's almost rudderless yet beautifully paced mid-afternoon set relegated any sartorial concerns to second place as they turned in a fantastic performance that simply made them.

And Queen weren't bad either.

There was no way Live 8 was going to re-create the same sort of global levels of clunky excitement as the original; things were much more professional by 2005 and a bit more boring for it. Plus, in the days since the first concert, we'd had 'cause' shows coming in from all sides, which of course kind of dulled the effect. But, as its principal players were at pains to point out, re-creating Live Aid wasn't really the idea, and as a bit of a sad old U2 fan I couldn't help but be enchanted to be so near the same four blokes exactly twenty years later as they prepared to open the show with a version of 'Sgt Pepper's Lonely Hearts Club Band', featuring none other than the song's original singer and co-author on guitar and lead vocals. I'm telling you, it was a real Text Your Dad moment.

Me and the rest of the Coldplay crew had the band's stuff set up and out of sight by 10 a.m., which would have been a lot more hassle without the help of various local crew members who had been especially booked to help set up, push equipment to the stage and get us anything we needed.

There are roadies all over the gaff at a time like this. Stagehands, drum technicians, lighting crews and even sweeper-uppers all swarm around each other, mostly in black and denim, like a scruffy little music army on rock 'n' roll battle manoeuvres. You'll also clock some instruments around the place that might make you gasp a bit – like Elton John's piano, for instance, which I walked past a number of times before realising what a legendary piece of kit I was failing to spot. Everything is set up on rolling risers for ease of movement, and each band has its own core team just like us lot. As usual there was a little friction and jostling for space – or 'real estate', as it's known – between crews, the securing of which normally depends on how much clout your bosses have and what levels of charm/surliness you're willing to display.

On this day we were lucky and got to use the revolving stage first, facing away from the audience on the unseen half (unlike twenty years before, the cheese at Live 8 was cut into two, not three) ready to rehearse the change-round from U2 to us which would later be happening in front of millions of people. There may have been men, motors or even ponies to pull the circular platform around for all I cared – my only concerns at that point were: (a) the potential for public technical catastrophe; and (b) how to get near some bacon, bread, ketchup and hot tea, ASAP. No one seemed to know where to find breakfast, and until Bono was happy and had got his rock star arse off the front stage we weren't going anywhere.

You simply aren't allowed to fuck this kind of show up, sandwich or no sandwich. There's scarcely any room for error and you're about as 'live' as you can be, so The Edge, Jonny Buckland or whoever had better have some noise and a guitar that's the right way round by the time he turns to face the world. It's a scarier responsibility for the crews than you might think, given that – as we've said – it isn't life or death, but trust me, no one wants to feel like a fool in front of that many onlookers and it only takes one stray wire to spoil the party. The band are pretty much placing their reputations in the crew's hands at this point and we just have to get on with it and try to get it right, whatever the circumstances.

Anyone who says they're never uptight and/or excited to be part of all this is going to have to buy me a pint and explain. OK, so we'd had fuck-all sleep, and there's always some annoying crap going down just to piss you off: U2's overlong soundcheck, for instance, redefined the concept of allotted time and seemed downright un-punk as far as our hungry roadie brains were concerned. Still, what are you going to do when the biggest group on the bill are rehearsing a tune with an ex-Beatle? It was tough shit, really, although we wouldn't have minded half as much if Larry Mullen Jr had just got off the drum kit for a minute, popped on an apron and brought us all a little snack.

But really, when you see the huge crowd properly for the first time and get hit by the cheer you just forget your troubles as any tensions get swept up and turned into a mean ball of adrenaline. It just makes you bristle and, unless you go running home to Mum, there's no avoiding the fact that pretty soon half the known world will be expecting to hear the sound of a guitar YOU tuned and an amp YOU plugged in.

So anyhow, U2 and Sir Paul *finally* wrapped things up and it was our turn. We had a brief line-check (like a mini soundcheck without the talent) of our own, which as usual involved me, Milly, Bash and Hoppy legging it around making sure that everything onstage was plugged in, working and capable of making a nasty racket. On this occasion, Will and Jonny came and had a tinkle too, but normally they wouldn't and if you've ever heard us roadies line-checking between bands, you'll know how ghastly it can be. Inept aural sludge at best and flash muso-noodling at worst, line-checking unfortunately serves a useful function. Put simply, each sound generated onstage, from the lead vocal right down to the bass drum, has to find its way to Danny at the FOH mixing desk and back to the big speakers or no one past Row 10 will hear more than a squeak. This is achieved by sending every pretty note/sonic horror through microphones or directly down loads of cables; these are the 'lines' you're checking, see? It's just like a great big hi-fi with Coldplay being the CD.

So, all was well. U2's backline faced the crowd, which by now was beginning to grow. Everything was ready at last, including the poncey, pink, pop-star-filled catering tent, which we ran at like recently landed sea-crazed pirates. There was no bacon, but we didn't care – we'd have eaten raw cabbage by then and, besides, there wasn't time to worry since before you knew it, Bono, Macca and the lads had opened the show and we were all stood back on the revolving cheddar, clutching guitars and drumsticks like rock sentries waiting for a riff invasion.

Nothing short of actually doing it can prepare any roadie for the moment a stage turns beneath them for the first time and a huge, expectant audience swings into full view, but everyone should get a go at it. It's completely mental, like the fairground ride of a lifetime. This is partly due to the rush you feel – a strange blend of exhilaration and suppressed terror – but you also quickly realise that despite the massive audience, cameras and all (which give you the fleeting sense that nothing exists, or is happening, anywhere else in the world) you're fundamentally alone in the middle of all this colossal intensity. There's nowhere to hide and it's literally just you, the lads, the equipment, the huge crowd, half a billion TV viewers and your mum's favourite bloody Beatle stood next to you clapping. If something fucks up – say, an amplifier starts making loud, farty noises in front of everybody – it's down to you to fix it, and your dad can't help you because he's at home watching it on the telly.

This one went well, mind, almost like clockwork, with no glitches I really noticed. The show was short, with a strong, stadium-paced 'In My Place' to start, after which Verve vocalist Richard Ashcroft came on and joined in for a splendid, preheated 'Bittersweet Symphony'. This was very cool, though I thought it broke the band's stride and threw the throng a bit; I wished in a way Coldplay had stuck to their own set. They finished with a warm, redemptive reading of 'Fix You' and left us (and, I suspect, themselves and the audience) feeling as though we'd all just woken from a strangely muted dream. The stage spun and we packed down extra quick, loaded up the vans, thanked the fantastic local stage crew for their help and made swiftly for RAF Northolt with the sound of Elton and Pete Doherty ringing in our ears.

The mood on the plane back was jolly in a 'job done' sort of way, despite the band's party *and* ours having been – check it out – delayed for another half an hour by good old U2 who'd arrived at the airfield slightly before us, fully laden and en route to rejoin their European tour. Chris, Jonny, Guy and Will, along with their immediate entourage of management, assistants and security people, then flew to Scotland separately, while everyone else on our flight laughed as me and Bash got scared during nasty turbulence on the way into Glasgow. I was so rattled that I even shouted, 'Fuck OFF! It's not funny!' at Milly for semi-inadvertently filming my distress, while Bash just made the usual frightened bear noises and pleaded with 'Biggles' to 'keep the nose up'.

A safe if bumpy landing, a mad race back to Bellahouston Park, and the world's fastest equipment setup were then followed by what was An Amazing Show without question. Crowds north of the border are, as we've said, well known for their mad enthusiasm and this was no exception. To use a shoddy cliché, the band seemed briefly at one with their fans (sorry, but there's no other way to put it), who lifted us all right up with the sheer power of an incredible reception. This was the sort of gig you only get once in a blue moon when a band is truly on fire, the audience is psyched to fuck and flying sparks just seem to weld it all together. The day had left everyone totally wired and Coldplay finished the job in fine, strident style, looking like a proper little gang of victorious fighters.

Nights and days like these make you remember why you loved gigs in the first place, and it was really satisfying to reflect as we packed up, drank beer and hopped onto the buses that somehow, since 1985, my big dream of being involved in top-flight rock 'n' roll had come true after all. Despite not actually having joined The Jam on bass or become the next Chris Stein, I was chuffed with where I was in the world and came out of our Live 8 day feeling sweaty, fried and happy, almost as if I'd been in Coldplay's front row myself.

CHAPTER TWELVE

WHAT DOES ENO ?
(RIFFS, STUDIOS AND OTHER FUN)

Being in a studio with the band is a totally different vibe from doing a gig – no more stamping about, getting sweaty and swearing for me (well, a bit less than normal at any rate). Also, with daily roars of mass approval being notably absent, the self-confidence levels of any half-successful outfit and its crew will gradually even out into a sort of gentle sine wave, punctuated occasionally by fleeting but powerful moments of euphoria and/or self-loathing. What with the considerable inter-personal tensions at play, lack of daylight and all-round absence of normality the whole process can get to feel a bit like a long raft ride down a bloody long, slow, bendy river.

My role in all this is fairly straightforward. During daily proceedings, if Jonny or anyone else happens to be in creative mode, I'll most likely have to be on hand to tune, mend or re-string guitars, but also I'm required to be fully available pretty much the whole time for fetching, carrying and setting up the various different chunks of studio backline equipment and sundry musical instruments. However, I'm not always based at the studio as quite often there are errands to do such as collecting necessary gear from the

'Task-saturated' PA-in-Chief Vicki Taylor dealing with multiple requests on two phones *and* a radio at Wembley, like she does every day on the road.

Guy then.

'Now … how the hell am I going to turn this pile of old cack
into a portable guitar rig?'
Author searches for clues at the Bakery, *Viva* sessions, 2007.

'Franksy, it's behind you!'
Bullet train, Japan, 2008.

'Er, chaps … are we sure about this new backdrop?'
Will goes urban, Midtown Manhattan, NYC *Today Show*, 2008.

'It'll sound different when the people come in.'
Danny stays calm, *Viva tour, 2008.*

'MAAAATT! HOPPEEE! BAAAASH! NEEEEIILLLL!'
Wembley Arena, London, June 2008.

'So, just to recap, the giant flying pig lands stage right during the first encore…'
Phil Harvey holds court, *Viva* rehearsals, Wembley Arena, March 2008.

The Boss backstage.
BBC TV Centre, London, June 2008.

Viva La Vida tour, Izod Center, New Jersey, October 2008.

'Thanks everybody. Goodnight!'
Viva tour, Izod Center, New Jersey, 2008.

band's well-stuffed lock-up or hunting down that rare, vintage mandolin or effects box someone fancies trying.

Not many roadies end up sticking with their bands between tours and this can actually be a brain-thumping time for most crew. Do you stay at home and rest? (Yes please.) And run out of dough? (No thanks.) Or go on the road again, with someone else? (Groan) Uh . . . maybe a bit of carpentry instead?

Everyone has to find their way, but chances are most of the other roadies won't see each other or work for Coldplay again until the next tour rolls around.

Yeah, I know. Jammy bastard. How the hell did I wangle it?

Well, as usual it's an estuary of a tale, with a great many tributaries, creeks and bridges. The first stream broke ground before the whole *X&Y* process even began as Jonny and I were having lunch at a North London rehearsal space. Looking up from his paper – and possibly not having considered the consequences – he simply said, 'Matt, can you show me how to set up all my equipment?'

Younger musicians or guitarists without a butler might chuckle at this, but it's not as simple as it sounds. We'd been out for eighteen months with *Rush of Blood*, the rig had got fairly complicated and by dint of constant touring and becoming a rock star etc., Jonny had never yet had cause to put it all together by himself.

'No problem,' I replied. 'Why?'

'Well, me and Chris are thinking of starting the next album together in Chicago.'

Cogs ahoy, I was on it like a panther.

'Really?' I said. 'Well whaddya say I come along too and help you both out?'

The glance we exchanged at this point reminded me of many other conspiratorial winks I've shared with people down the years, like when you and your mate decide to bunk off school and get pissed on cheap cider by the river.

'All right,' Jonny replied, grinning. 'I'll have a word.'

A few days later I found myself in London Heathrow's BA Executive Lounge, scheduled to board a daytime flight to Illinois. In the time since our little chat, Jonny had somehow convinced everyone that he couldn't possibly tune his own guitars at the studio and, therefore, I should obviously be offered a fortnight in a posh suite at the Four Seasons Hotel on full wages. Having flown Club Class (which is always a nice treat, but back then a right novelty as well) Jonny and I were met at O'Hare Airport by two large dudes in shades and suits, whose job it was to – get this – show us to the bloody car. After a twenty-minute Lincoln limo ride, we were walked separately to our fancy, high-rise rooms by some fairly fawning hotel staff who took great delight in showing us the rock star view and explaining where the twee bog was. Once left alone, I took a breath, looked out over the twinkly city lights and wondered how lucky a West Country punk rocker could get.

Chicago is an amazing town. It's right on a massive lake for a start, which is cool, and the skyline looks about as Batman as it gets. Historically a tough frontier melting pot, the Windy City also boasts one of the most finely honed drinking cultures I've yet encountered, with which Jonny and I became reacquainted almost immediately as, lit by a golden autumn, the town's central area became our night-time playpen for a full fortnight. Chris would vacate the studio at around sundown to hook up with Gwyneth (who was filming a daylight-hours-only shoot further up the block), leaving us in the mischievous and capable hands of our two local studio assistants, Mackie and Frenchy, who it's fair to say really ought to have got out of the recording business and written their own 'Find A Bar That's Open in Chicago, NOW!' guidebook.

I've rarely been so regularly drunk, or hungover, in my life. Never mind New York or any other town, this is the real one that never sleeps – or, to be more precise, doesn't know when it's time to pack it in. Chewing our way through late-night dives like a pair of hungry caterpillars, Jon and I once got so messed up that getting back to the hotel without a cab proved a complete physical impossibility, even though we could see at least two of it. The frolic potential seemed infinite, but as ever with fun and games of any sort, there was a price to pay. Each morning around 9 a.m., a fit, rested and restored Chris Martin would bound into the studio, brimming with ideas, volume and energy, and pretty much holler the words, 'Hi, fellas. What's the matter?'

It's to Jon's credit that he managed to get through each creative session at all, let alone come up with any riffs. Still, the studio bond was sealed between us all and, amazingly enough, I ended up being offered a full, regular post on proper money.

Once back on home turf and with the Coldplay rhythm section recalled, the whole band began flitting from studio to studio in a half-desperate, half-casual attempt to hunt down the spark that lit up the *Rush of Blood* sessions so decisively a couple of years before. I spent some weeks with them at Liverpool's Parr Street, which actually bore more boozy headaches than musical fruit largely thanks to the presence of an adjoining bar that never, ever seemed to shut. It was a strange time, during which I actually found myself behind the kit in a semi-drunk, post-pub jam situation with sundry Coldplay members and Scouse legend Ian McCulloch, who, doubtless just to completely freak me out, wore shades, sang lead vocals and strummed along with us on a vintage Gibson 335. Blimey – go back to 1982 and tell that one to my teenage Echo And The Bunnymen-adoring self.

It's probably worth taking a moment, while I'm here, to discuss the whole recording process, just in case anyone doesn't quite get it. I'm not going to delve very deeply into the nuts and bolts – it's all way too technical and doubtless a bit boring for a lot of readers – but if as a kid you ever managed to get your own joke/burp/fart down onto a worn cassette and marvel at how funny the playback sounded, then you should be aware of the basic appeal. Multiply the art, science and expense levels of this simple experiment by a few hundred thousand and, hey presto, you're in a modern recording studio, possibly with Coldplay! Now, at last, you can record your nice juicy belch properly.

There's no real 'correct' way to bash a recorded work into shape. Kraftwerk's methods probably wouldn't have worked for Led Zep, for instance – you'd never have got John Bonham to spend ten minutes whapping out a basic beat on a prototype, home-built synth drum, nor Ralf Hütter to fly off to Mordor on a cranked Les Paul Custom. But there are similarities. You're basically after the same sort of sonic thing, which is to say there'll probably be percussion, some kind of bass line, a main riff and a melody. Beyond that, it's into the silly zone really – sometimes drums go down first, sometimes everything at once, sometimes the guitar part . . . there are so many ways to attack it it'd be misleading to take just one tune and describe its entire gestation. But at the end of the day, what makes most modern recording possible is the (now) old and simple process of overdubbing – which some readers might not have a clue about.

You can, by the wonders of technology, record the guitar, then the bass, then wipe the guitar off, then put the tin whistle on, then change the levels of everything and sing over it all separately, on another day or whenever you like. I know, it's amazing, isn't it? I thought when I was a kid that the Beatles just went in and did 'Strawberry Fields' in one go, and that there must be about thirty of them. *Tubular Bells* killed that idea. One bloke playing all those parts, how the fuck did he do that? I was confused for about five years, until someone explained the idea of multitracking to me and that Mike Oldfield wasn't just legging it round the studio really fast between instruments, like a one-man orchestra.

With all this in mind, it might be worth debating whether or not a lot of recording techniques have become almost a bit over-clever in recent times. Some traditionally minded studio folks gripe that super-modern equipment doesn't actually help much in the long run, citing the physical and artistic limitations imposed by older, more basic facilities as positive factors when it comes to producing a cool-sounding record. Others might counter that the opposite is true, since loads of great albums have been defined by technology and are, without question, each the end product of a massive, protracted chin-stroke. Actually, when you look at it, a good few of the world's best-loved recorded works have come from a mixture of both schools, forged during those rare times when artists and machines seem to fan each other's flames, pushing the whole project far out into uncharted waters. (There's a line to be drawn here from *Sgt*

Pepper through *Dark Side Of The Moon* and on to the early Streets'
material and beyond via The White Stripes' *De Stijl*, but I can't be
arsed and you'd only laugh.) Still, regardless of where anyone's
sensibilities lie, the creative chain of events in studios largely unfolds
as follows:

1) Person has idea. Decides for him/herself if it's any good.
2) Shows colleague, who may encourage or trash whole
   notion, depending.
3) All hands present attempt to twist, coax and wheedle
   original concept into tidy, recorded compliance. This
   might be easy, but is more likely to be about as awkward
   as dressing a really wriggly baby.
4) Results assessed.
5) Instigator happy/fed up.
6) Hit/flop occurs.

Of course, there's a good deal more to the process than this and it
can take minutes, days, weeks or sometimes months for even the
strongest musical bean to sprout any roots. Much depends on your
production team's skill in the mad art of band steering, not to
mention said group's ability to hold fast while still bending with the
tune's breeze. It's amazing to ponder how many potential 'Let It Be's
or 'Paranoid's might have stalled during these early moments; for
instance, 'Viva La Vida' itself came perilously (and, in light of the live
anthem it became, unthinkably) close to being trashed completely
due to a few key people's initial dislike of it. And Coldplay's
ultimately show-stopping opus 'Fix You' – the only song to make it
from *X&Y* onto the entire *Viva* tour relatively unaltered – might

never have seen the light of day had Chris given up and caved in when Guy politely asked of him at London's legendary-but-now-gone Townhouse Studios one morning: 'So, "tears stream down your face, and AAAAH". What's that all about, then?'

Tricky.

But perhaps not as tricky as getting what they call 'a good performance' down on tape. Sometimes, if it's not quite happening, everyone will leg it out of the studio to give the artiste in question a bit of quiet time to perform with the lights out, or occasionally a close colleague might have to gee them up a bit and pretend to be 20,000 people at a gig in order to promote some extra vitality. Hilarious and intense in equal measure, but it's true to say that more than a few choice musical moments have been conjured up this way. When someone weighs in with a defining musical part, the vibes in a studio can be just lovely, making it all suddenly worth the grind, like the time a happy cheer went up as Guy conceived his final, locked-down, spunky bass riff for 'Speed of Sound'. These are the things that can stick in the heart, make the whole gang smile again and really pull everyone forward.

However, as any act from The E-Street Band right down will surely concur, it doesn't matter where you are or what you spend, sometimes you just can't force it. On returning to London following the Parr Street sessions and with more than a year's work behind them, it soon became apparent that even Air Studios (owned at the time by Beatles production deity George Martin and – noticeably – situated in a very large church) couldn't wring the magic out of Coldplay. We had a few five-a-side footy matches in the car park and re-learned the *Grandstand* theme but, despite everyone's best efforts, things just weren't quite right.

Sparing zero expense, the band decided to take the search (and me) to Manhattan for a month, kipping at the swanky 'W' hotel, Union Square, and working by day at Hell's Kitchen's also legendary-but-now-gone studio The Hit Factory. In the end, the enviable facilities and opulent digs only hatched one finished song, but it was probably worth it: 'Til Kingdom Come' survived these sessions and made it onto *X&Y* in the live, Wild West form it was recorded, with Will stony-faced at the pump organ and Guy rocking some deep bass notes on a big black grand piano. In between the band's other attempted assaults on the elusive summit successfully scaled by the likes of 'Clocks' and 'Politik', we all ate sushi and played cricket in the huge live room using a tennis ball and a homemade bat – happy hours without doubt, but in the end something had to break. We packed up the wicket, grabbed our bags and headed back to London.

There were a few tough old weeks left ahead, during which time Coldplay switched producers, hopped between studios and each band member in turn came to question the merit of all they'd done so far, amid tabloid rumours that if the album didn't get finished by a certain date, Dennis Quaid would have to be called in to save EMI shareholders from a second ice age. The very process of creating a body of recorded music (repeated listening, separate parts being put down as overdubs rather than as part of an ensemble, etc.) can kill perspective and hamper any band's efforts to pull things together in a cohesive way, which might affect inspiration levels and, in turn, the buoyancy of the whole project. For me though, one of music's chief joys comes from never quite knowing when the magic's going to return, and really all I can do at my end is try to be useful, not get in the way and hopefully help things along a little by putting in the occasional constructive comment, cheeky remark or . . . riff!

If you're near a copy of *X&Y* and can be bothered to get up, have a look at the notes on the inside sleeve. You'll see a little sentence, about halfway down – next to Brian Eno's synth credit, mark you – that reads: 'X1 has a guitar riff by Matt McGinn.'

How cool is that? What the hell happened?

Well, it's funny really, with riffs. I've made up, loved and copied so many down the years you'd think I'd be sick of them, but they're still the musical component I dig the most. If you like rock 'n' roll at all you'll already know how a really good one at the right volume can slay your worries, get you off your arse and make you feel really powerful, as though you just threw open some curtains and raised the sash windows in a dingy old house. Think of your favourites: 'Johnny B Goode', 'Brown Sugar', 'God Save The Queen', 'Enter Sandman', 'Sex Machine'; the list is as long as you like, but how does the alchemy actually happen? It's a miracle, right?

Search me for the details, I'm not a musicologist. I've no idea why when David Bowie's 'The Jean Genie' strikes up its primordial stomp I suddenly feel like I could defeat whole gangs of thugs unarmed, or why the last guitar bit of 'The Scientist' makes everyone want to cry regardless of what Chris might have been singing about prior to its chimely arrival. For my part, it's been said that there were church bells ringing nearby when I was born, the regimented, repetitive and dare I say tidy cycle of which might easily have had some early musical bearing. In any event, silly though it sounds, riffs eventually came to define some sort of central focus for me which – incredibly – survived until one fairly ordinary day almost forty years later when I found myself alone in the live room of Trevor Horn's West London studio attempting to console a thoroughly despondent Chris Martin, who, with only weeks to go until *X&Y*'s original deadline, had once again burrowed himself into an especially dark mid-afternoon warren.

'It's crap, Matt. The album's rubbish.'

Oh dear.

'What's up, man?' I asked. There was music playing through some discarded headphones nearby and, like any annoying old guitar twat, I'd started to noodle along. 'What are you unhappy about?'

It didn't matter. Suddenly distracted, Chris looked up.

'What's that?'

'Oh, nothing. I dunno. What tune are we hearing?'

'It's new. Might be called "Square One". That's a cool riff!'

'Cheers.'

'Can we have it?'

'Er, yeah, of course.'

Coldplay fans (or anyone else reading, come to that) could be forgiven for gasping out loud at this point. I mean, the levels on which Chris's request might have rocked one's world are various, not least of which being the fact that, for a start, it's a massive compliment from a hugely successful riff lover/writer.

Here's the other thing, though. Whether or not you're in a band, if you happen to write, or help write, a bit of music that then gets recorded and/or published, you're really meant to get some extra money. For whatever reason, there's a bucket-load of spare cash set aside for songwriters that you won't get your hands on by just playing on a record. Simple, eh?

If sodding only. Sad to have to relate here that the history of recorded music is littered with financial casualties who didn't get their fair dues, for a wide variety of pitiful reasons. Some early victims had no idea how much their tunes might be worth in years to come and were thus completely exploited, while others have fallen prey down the decades to unscrupulous, selfish or plain mean colleagues who simply kept the whole cake for themselves. OK, so not everyone's in rock 'n' roll for the money – heaven knows there are easier ways to make a few quid – but it's kind of sad to contemplate the fate of all those sidekicks who rode the biggest wave only to be dumped on the beach without a board, let alone a ride home, especially considering that without them there'd have been no fucking surf in the first place.

It's much nicer, of course, to think of the happy tales. Bono Vox, for example, might well have written most of U2's classic, signature, sing-along choruses, while The Edge's best guitar bits are quite rightly known and celebrated throughout the musical world, but you have to hand it to them both for openly appreciating and acknowledging that without the other two members, there wouldn't have been any group at all. For a start, drummer Larry Mullen Jr was famously the cat responsible for putting the first 'Musicians Wanted' ad up in their school corridor, while bassist Adam Clayton went on to prove invaluable as a polite, confident hustler who secured them their first gigs and then – crucially – found the band an inspired manager. But, perhaps most importantly of all, despite the odds and for technical reasons that could take all night to explain, within a few cool years these two somehow managed to go from being cack-handed school kids to clocking in as one of the most sonically dramatic, propulsive rhythm sections of the late twentieth century. For these and a hundred other reasons, U2 royalties are split very fairly indeed.

OK, you could say that things are easier for them – true, it's a big old basket of fish and loaves this mob are sharing out. But really, bollocks to all that. The point is that they've probably always done it and I'm willing to bet that they, and groups like them, were getting their round in way before the first song was even written. Coldplay certainly were, right from the day we met (remember Chris thanking me for playing football with him?) and, to my knowledge, nothing's really changed along the way; this is the sort of group that would take their guitar roadie's riff, twist it a bit, play it themselves on the song, still credit the person involved *and* slice them a chunk of the profits for good measure.

Not bad, is it?

Well, anyway, somehow *X&Y* got finished, thank heavens, and turned out pretty damn fine as well considering its rather unstable gestation period. I suffered a nasty viral invasion later on and missed a chunk of the final stages, but I still recall the studio stress levels nudging more than slightly into the red. Bands often get nervous about finishing a record, partly because it's such a big deal knowing they're shortly going to be so thoroughly judged, added to which everyone, from the label boss to their nan's long-lost cousin, starts arriving at the studio, all bringing their well-meaning, helpful opinions on how best to wrap it all up. Which is all the more distracting when you're trying really hard to nail that last-minute guitar solo on 'A Message'.

Still, no pain, no gain. Luckily for everyone, the band and their tunes were tough enough to withstand the ruck, though Jonny has said since that getting the final mix for 'Speed of Sound' right was one of the most challenging things they'd thus far achieved as a recording outfit. This, like a lot of studio triumphs and disasters, was for reasons of a sonic and technical nature that might, if explored, nudge the average reader a bit too far into muso territory for comfort. It was worth all the effort in the end though, and as soon as I heard the finished track for the first time on Chris Moyles's radio show I got a sudden and overwhelming feeling that everything was going to turn out OK. Which it pretty much did, when you think about it: best-selling album worldwide of 2005, third fastest selling LP in UK chart history, darkest blue outer sleeve of all time, etc.

How much bands like Coldplay relish the thought of going back into the studio after a big tour, and why, could be a subject for much debate. After a year or more on the road it's usual to hear most musicians saying stuff like 'Can't wait to get off the road and start recording' or 'I'm bored shitless of groupies, let's get some new tunes done, for fuck's sake!', almost as if they've blotted out, like new mums, how much sheer aggro the birth really was.

With this in mind, midway through the *Twisted Logic* carnival, someone near the core of things – no one quite remembers who, or wants to take the credit – had the bright idea of building the band their own little workspace back home. Well, why not? Quality studio time in London has always carried the world's daftest price tag, so why donate all that hard-earned dough to someone else's yacht fund? Just a little place to write tunes, mess about and hang in was all they needed. Cheap 'n' cheerful, you know? Nothing fancy.

Months of planning, building and much collective grief later, the band was sitting pretty as their pathological inability to do things by halves had brought them a beautiful, state-of-the-art baby studio, complete with offices, showers, big sofas, wooden floors and even a white spiral staircase.

For those who've not had the pleasure, most recording facilities are odd places, often sporting little or no natural light and, as a result, having a boxed-in sort of vibe. But not this gaff. Either by luck, judgement or a bit of both, our new base was the complete opposite – open, light and friendly – despite its actual recording space being not much larger than your average-sized posh London flat. Part of the beauty of the place was the whole multilevel thing, which meant that if, say, Jonny and Will felt like getting away from the music they could just leg it upstairs to the big lounge and play footy on Nintendo, or whatever the kids are into these days. The soundproofing between floors never quite got finished in time so people on the third (office) level would have to put up with loud drums or bass now and then, but not to any crippling extent and, as we always say, if that's as bad as your day gets then you're doing all right. It was such a luxury to suddenly have a place where everything stayed set up and ready to go that sometimes I'd get to work really early, turn on, tune up and do nothing but sit there for twenty minutes, either playing guitar through the fancy gear or just looking around and thinking 'Wow', with a cup of tea and a bacon sandwich.

The whole thing was quite gorgeous, and the timing was pretty lovely too – once we'd all got off the road after *Twisted Logic* wound up in Japan, me and my girl bought our first house just in time to join the rapidly growing Coldplay & Associates Parents' Circle, and after a decade of intense flying, insane bedtimes and long, long drives I could hardly believe my luck as I found myself actually cycling to work each morning like some old denim-clad village bobby.

With tour manager Franksy casting a parental eye over daily

proceedings, and tireless assistants Vicki and EJ aboard, the 'Bakery' as it was becoming known (after a previous incarnation of the premises) began to feel like a proper little hive of family activity, like a sort of rock 'n' roll Walton's Mountain with poncey smoothies and salami ciabattas instead of corn chowder and lemonade.

Soundman Danny stayed on as a general all-round useful dude, good vibes source and extra-curricular knob twiddler, quickly earning himself the superhero name 'Signal Path Boy' in honour of his amazing ability to tell, at a glance, why things weren't making any noise. Someone wise hired Andy 'Tall' Rugg as our in-house studio helper, I was allowed to stick around for some reason, and hardy-perennial-cum-fifth-member Phil Harvey took on the dangerous but vital role of Visiting Creative Consultant, a sanity-defying post of extreme stress and importance which involved, among other things, showing up from time to time and telling everyone what he thought of the music. (Anyone who thinks this sounds easy should pop their face into a live snakes' nest for five minutes sometime and get back to me.) Rik Simpson, a skilled and peaceful young man given to bouts of excessive coping, became our full-time recording engineer/co-producer while top German producer/ex-gymnast Markus Dravs arrived soon after, bringing some much-needed military PT-ground flavour and sideways humour to the proceedings. With the occasional addition of various visiting musicians, piano tuners and cleaners, the team was complete and we were under way . . . hang on, I've forgotten somebody!

Let's not fuck around here. I may well have been credited alongside him for contributing to *X&Y* but when I heard this man would be joining us for the fourth album it caused great ripples of excitement, not least of all in my mother who, if you recall, changed a few lives forever by bringing home his first proper album when I was only seven years old.

Roxy Music's eponymous debut had, along with four or five equally bonkers recorded works of the time, such a seismic effect on my pre-teen mind that the net results are impossible to quantify. (These people were up against some stiff competition, considering the first single I ever bought was 'Hey Rock 'n' Roll' by Showaddywaddy.) Whatever you might think of this mad bunch of tunes now – and I do suggest you check it out – there's no denying the simple fact that the far-out, twisted collages he and his five incomparable bandmates put forth back in the dark dawn of the 1970s fired sonic shards and wild imagery so far into my young psyche that none of it shows signs of dislodging, even today. Add to that some of his later work (U2's *Joshua Tree* and Bowie's *Heroes* for starters) and you'll start to get an idea of the size of arena we were about to enter.

So, bearing that – and my tendency towards star-stricken swooning – in mind, I can tell you it was a nervous old pedaller that parked his pushbike in the Bakery lobby on the morning of Brian Eno's arrival. I'd met him before, but only briefly and anyway it was a whole different vibe. This time, I was going to be *working* with the geezer.

The core issue bothering me that day was a simple one: despite having thumbed a ride up through the hairpins to somewhere near the top of my profession, I still felt like a kid stuck up a fucking tree. What if a real, live, big hitter like Brian came along and, having formed deep bonds in the past with the likes of Edge and his roadie (my hero) Dallas Schoo, spotted little me out there, quivering like a lost robin at the end of my bendy branch?

The truth is, it's never worth the worry, since few of us are ever really alone with this stuff. Chris, for example, who as we've seen is: (a) pretty successful; and (b) generally a man ready and willing to tackle new challenges, showed up for his first proper day's work looking focussed but a bit nervy, and who's to say Eno wasn't feeling that way too as he entered our little den? As it turned out, we needn't have been concerned at all since on his arrival Brian immediately radiated such warmth, good humour and positivity we almost became – get this – chilled out. I'd like to think we gave him and Markus a friendly welcome too, and all in all it didn't take long before we'd fallen into the classic men-on-a-raft patterns of joke-telling, ribbing and storytelling that actually characterise life on a tour bus.

Both our new producers endeared themselves to everyone early on in different ways; Brian's love of bawdy humour and fine yarns mixed well with his fierce, deliberate pursuit of ideas, while Markus's practical, no-nonsense approach and fearless honesty sometimes spilled into sheer comic genius.

Hilarious exchanges, particularly with Coldplay's perma-questioning front man, soon became commonplace as everyone chased the elusive muse and tried to keep a hold of their shaky footing all at once. Here's a classic that reared its head one lunchtime during the early hours of the then proto-metal monster 'Violet Hill's ultimately healthy lifespan:

Chris (approaching end of tether): 'Why are you so down on this song, Markus? Your view of it is so depressing!'

Markus (with many yards of tether to spare): 'That's not me, it's your paranoia.'

Then, after a pause . . . 'Are you on drugs?'

One of the band's wishes at the outset of recording was for what became *Viva La Vida* to be forged in the heat of the live room – where all the loud stuff is, drums, guitars and stuff, as opposed to the control room, which houses the mixing desk and sundry recording devices.

With the daftness and sheer omnipotence of modern technology it's quite possible to make a perfectly good, even brilliant album without much real interplay between the band members. But on the whole, groups like Coldplay – who even their haters should admit are at the very least a highly effective musical unit – often do best when things are cooking between them and the vibe is really collective. To this end, new activities such as 'Musical Gym' – a novel, improvisational pursuit intended to flex the creative muscles which involved the group being actually conducted by Brian or Markus – were introduced, with quite positive, often inspiring and occasionally hilariously cacophonous results.

This sort of 'anything's worth a try' attitude doesn't make for a speedy recording process but certainly ensures that no stone gets left unturned. Some mornings, for instance, Guy would arrive early and just start playing bass on his own. Whoever showed up next might decide to join in, followed by another, until by elevenses you'd have a full-on jam taking place, all of which would get recorded and noted down just in case anything inspiring had happened. I remember running into the control room a few times and saying to Rik in a stage whisper, 'Quick, press go, Berryman's playing a cool riff!'

If good things developed from there on you'd feel a little warm glow inside, as if maybe that day you'd really helped them all along. This was definitely the case one dark, wintry afternoon when Chris suddenly said, 'Matt, let's go and buy a terrible piano!' We all put on our big jackets and fucked off down to the local store in Kentish Town where – not before the boss had brought the house down with a breezy 'Hello, we'd like to purchase your worst instrument' – he tried a cheap one out and coughed up a few hundred quid for it. We then brought it home in a van, stuck drawing pins on the beaters inside and within a few days the lad was racing between corners of the studio, like my imagined Mike Oldfield, trying to explain to everyone how the three separate musical movements of new song '42' were going to fit together.

The inevitable technical and logistical problems kept us busy as well – just like with touring, someone's computer/amplifier/banjo always seemed to be exploding at the crucial moment (often Brian would be nearby when this happened . . . hmm, spooky/magnetic) and despite the Bakery being armed to the teeth with top gear it was invariably that fallow, corroding piece of old shite we'd put right at the back of the lock-up that they suddenly really needed. This came to be my cue for many a frantic call to Hoppy, who by some weird quirk of quiffy *Back to the Future* magic always knew exactly where to find, say, the faulty kazoo Will had once played long, long ago on the B-side to 'Bigger Stronger'.

'Yeah, I know that one. It's under Chris's old electric piano behind all the empty guitar cases in Cage Seven.'

Of course there were plenty of other times when nothing needed shifting around, plugging in or mending and myself, Danny or Andy were left with an embarrassing lack of things to do. The only thing for it then was to all hide away in my guitar world out the back by the kitchen, drink tea and talk pedals/politics while big debates raged and theories abounded beyond the glass, until Markus would suddenly burst into our little space and say,

'Matt, we need a theremin and a balalaika. This afternoon. Would you mind seein' to it?'

One thing I didn't get involved with though, was Brian's inspired/unhinged idea of bringing in a hypnotist to see what tunes everyone would come up with while balancing bananas on their heads and taking their trousers off (OK, I'm joking about the bananas). Cushions were arranged, lights were dimmed and eyes were closed for quite some time and, as anyone who's been through proper hypnotherapy will understand, things became exceedingly relaaaaaaaxed.

The net effect was actually quite interesting. Usually a tense hive of joy, angst, loud noise and collective struggle, the Bakery (and its principal gang of inhabitants) suddenly got almost silent and weirdly tranquil. After a little while, music was played – pretty gently, as I recall – on various instruments but stopped short of the expected whale-noises and may well have inspired some of what came later, particularly in the sonic-soundscape department. OK, it's not a very punk-rock approach, but Will has said since that for days afterwards he felt quite positive about everything and that it really helped his confidence.

Other points in the project were a bit less than Zen, particularly when it was decided that we'd shift proceedings half a mile up the street to Air Studios, for the sake of a change of scene as much as anything else. This massive musical ark, beloved of many big bands and orchestras thanks to its stained glass windows, huge live rooms, top-flight service and abundance of nice staff, came to feel like a listing hulk at times as various Coldplay people worked on different songs in separate parts of the building and then came together to dissect and try to add to each other's efforts, often in a less than productive way. The vibe was getting a bit shaky and, after a few brave stabs at finishing things off, people started to drift back to the safety and all-round buzziness of our little home down the hill.

Of course, the tensions of band life will follow you everywhere, especially when time's marching by and you haven't actually finished the string parts on 'Viva La Vida' yet, let alone decided if it's going to be on the album at all (and eventually become your biggest ever smash hit). Funny how things turn out; a year or more later, having been given its own special tour, the song would seem to swell up with defiant pride as the crowd joined in for the final, euphoric, football terrace yell-along as I stood smiling to myself under the stage thinking, fuck me, I was right there when they wrote this. And it so nearly went in the dustbin!

Still, something about the Bakery atmosphere seemed to agree with everyone as the last recordings began to bleed into other stuff, like meetings with set designers, press interviews, on-site costume designing, instrument decorating and darts matches, most of which took place above us while we tried desperately to get the live equipment back into shape in time downstairs. For instance, we had meetings galore and grew many a headache trying to make Jonny's guitar setup just right, and it ended up costing him and the band tens of thousands but, as you'll have hopefully already read in the 'Gig Day' chapter, we ended up with a fabulous, practical, sonically enviable rig that was only ever really let down by outside factors such as climate and/or human error. Neill and Miller spent long hours soldering and tinkering with live keyboard options while I got to grips with the rudiments of guitar radio technology and how to fix RF transmitters to guitar straps. It almost felt a bit like a real old Bakery for a while, or at least a busy little cottage textiles factory.

Before you knew it, it was time to repaint the live room, set up for gig rehearsals and meet Fin, our new production manager.

Then, in one incredible moment, Chris turned to Danny and me on the way out the door and said, 'Great job, fellas. *Viva La Vida* is ready. Let's get out of here.'

Fuck me, here we go again . . .

CHAPTER THIRTEEN

THE HOME STRAIGHT

So the big engine spluttered back into life. All the necessary backline kit was cased up and loaded out of the Bakery, pushed down the alleyway between the estate agents and the bistro and out onto a big silver truck bound for Wembley Arena, which had been booked solid for two weeks' worth of production rehearsals. A whole host of old roadie faces reappeared and an army of fresh ones showed up for the first time, saying 'hi' in strange new voices that became super-familiar within days and sounded as comfy as my mum's by the summer. Some, like me, didn't sleep for a week just from excitement and worry but the mood was upbeat, if a tad stressy. Stages were built, torn down, rebuilt. Ideas came. Ideas went. And came back again. Pricey, custom kit got trashed because it looked shit. Early casualties on the *Viva* tour included the original, light-reflective, beige plastic stage covering, along with an odd-looking, raised, slightly wobbly circular electric railway that had been painstakingly carped for lights and cameras to encircle the band on. Video content went in the bin, songs were dropped, then returned. Tears of anguish, joy and relief were shed daily in all departments, which made the whole thing as vibey, scary and exciting as your first school nativity, just with more roadies, less shepherds and a slightly bigger budget.

Before we set off for the wilds of the open road, the band – wisely, we all felt – decided to invite a few hundred selected friends and family along to the arena so they could have a look at the show as it stood. There's nothing like a crowd, related or not, to get things pumping and really shine a light on what works and what doesn't so, with Franksy putting in a fine turn as ringmaster and MC, off we went into what might have felt to us like the clunkiest Coldplay show ever, but probably wasn't. Put it this way, my mum, dad, girlfriend and mates all really loved it so it seemed we were off to a fair start.

It's a tough birthing process for any Coldplay tour. They can take weeks, even months, of trial and error to nail into shape, much of which will happen in the full glare of the audience's headlights way before the thing gets anywhere near to being anything like the massive rock 'n' roll ball of snow it's destined to become. America and Europe whizz past in a blur of daily changes, crazy routing and TV promo appearances, and the general feeling is a long way from settled, sorted or anything like confident. But, before we knew it and what seemed like moments later, a whole year had gone by and we were working for the undisputed biggest, baddest thing on the planet that was kicking arse so hard we could hardly believe it ourselves. It's funny, there's usually a dip in the proceedings just before this happens – like a lull in the weather – and *Viva La Vida* was no exception; somewhere just past its centenary show, we hit a short, nasty American run which culminated in Chris coming to grief on a greasy, post-storm outdoor stage and getting burned by some live pyro. He fell over quite hard in front of one of the few non-sold out crowds of the tour, following which the lad promptly got sick enough to actually cancel a show, something we've only seen happen three or maybe four times in ten years.

Still, it's another measure of the fighting spirit in evidence around here that immediately following this nadir, the band – and crew – got off the mat and came back bigger and tougher than ever, pumped up in no small part by the sheer brass and quality of the support acts. On the midsummer US *Viva* run of 2009, gorgeous, blessed openers Howling Bells were followed by the mighty, grinning Snow Patrol, whose music I didn't even like all that much until they showed up and politely knocked us sideways with their all-round niceness and generally relaxed, professional attitude (I'm including their crew here). All smiles, they cooked their 40-minute warm-up slot to perfection and grabbed the audience with both hands, a bit like Coldplay did when they supported Muse all those chapters ago . . . with similar hair and trousers!

With all this going on out in the house as they warmed up their voices backstage and got into the costumes, Chris, Jon, Guy and Will couldn't help but come out punching and tear into the arenas like sharks on a feeding frenzy, putting us all right back on top of the game in a matter of days. It was fantastic and cool as fuck to be up close to and involved with a show that had so much spunk and vigour; this was a band performing right out of its skin and you couldn't help but be stoked about what was coming next . . .

Everyone's so burned towards the end of a world tour it's not funny. Band, management, crew, everyone. But, just as we're all about to keel over into our Beck's, here comes the hugest thing any of us original old Coldplay gits have ever done, bar none. Let me try to explain.

People had been quietly planning this shit for months, but suddenly, almost without warning, a hundred new faces, umpteen more buses and eleventy-three trucks arrived. We'd already done way over 100 shows on four continents in front of more than two million people, but now we were stepping up a gear: seventeen massive outdoor European dates spread out over four weeks, finishing with two shows at – whisper it – Wembley.

So, why play a stadium? Rock 'n' roll cash experts tell me there's more money to be made in the sheds. Theatres are more fun, arenas are drier and less windy. Small clubs are way cooler. And unless you spend a wad of dough on a massive production, even the smallest giant outdoor sports venue will make your band – arena performances and big tunes honed beautifully or not – look and sound like a bunch of ants. Not to mention the logistics; few stadia were ever built with gigs in mind so the load-ins are often challenging at best, with drivers having to park trucks half a mile from the stage and armies of crew wheeling kit in on forklifts or by hand. And it's a half-hour hike to catering.

But so what? You still would, wouldn't you? Even the Sex Pistols and The Clash, leaders of the charge against inflated old rubbish back in the day, ended up playing Crystal Palace and Shea Stadium respectively, just like everyone before them that they promised they'd come to destroy. And, frankly, why the hell not? Bruce Springsteen once said he resisted the massiveness for years, but then realised if he didn't go for it, he'd have regretted it all his life.

I've never asked my bosses what led them to make a similar choice. No need, is there?

Stadium tours aren't like normal, i.e. you don't just go from place to place with everything and everybody. So much more kit needs setting up for each concert that if the whole production just travelled here and there like a circus you'd end up with a week or more between shows. So, put simply, you have three main stages; one that's used for the actual gig, one getting simultaneously put up in the next town and one being torn down in the last. Each stage setup has its own power generators and full advance crew – including caterers, production and IT experts – and gets carted around in about fifteen massive artics. So, with our travelling kit – that's the PA, lights, video gear, backline, front of house and everything that stays with us for each show – you're looking at around fifty trucks in total. The travelling crew's transport fleet has grown from four buses to eight, so at ten or twelve roadies per bus, that's a lot of people, and we're not even adding in the extra crew on advance and rearguard duties here, which probably doubles the number, if not more.[11]

Silkeborg. It sounds like a men's hair product from the 1970s, doesn't it? Probably as advertised by a Scandinavian tennis genius. But no, it's a little town nestled right in the middle of Denmark's foresty interior, surrounded by lakes, trees and not a whole lot else. Still bent out of shape having just finished the final North American leg of the *Viva* tour, us backline boys were dropped there in August 2009 and hung out for a day or two while hundreds of exhausted roadies – some of whom had flown straight out of Miami and right into work – tried to finish building *Viva*'s first stadium-sized gig in time for the band to show up and practise.

---

[11] Chances are we in the backline crew won't ever meet most of them, though, like ships that pass in the shite.

Sorry to have to relate here that (riggers, carps and everyone else look away now) I had a pretty nice time during the early part of that week cycling through the woods with my girlfriend, hanging about the town and drinking beer, virtually oblivious to the magnitude of the task that was taking place a short shuttle ride away.

Silkeborg's show (which was actually sort of nowhere, near another town called Herning) took place, like a few others on the stadium run including the next one in Bergen, Norway, in what are called 'green field sites', basically a festival-type arrangement but with fewer bands and a bigger headline production. These are nice for the outdoor crowds as each show feels like the fans' own exclusive little Glastonbury, with burger vans, silly hats and lots of trees you can disappear into for a pee, snog or whatever.

The downside is that us lot are left a bit exposed to the weather, which blew and occasionally rained at us for most of the Silkeborg production week in big, bothersome gusts like some drunk bastard in the pub who keeps prodding you and wanting your attention. Without the shelter of an actual stadium, the wet can get blown into your onstage equipment pretty effectively so you've got to be ready with big sheets of thick plastic, or 'Visqueen', cut to the right size to quickly cover up the amps, drums and keyboards. While electric guitars themselves generally respond poorly to excessive moisture, quickly becoming difficult to play and sounding like dull cack, it's much safer to be on radio packs than cables in the wet since you're not physically connected to the big, scary power truck. If it rains on the pedal boards though (which is more likely, since they sit right up at the main downstage lip), it's not good for the works so we'll cover them with see-through plastic that's movable enough for the pedals to still be useable during the inevitable wet periods. These followed us so doggedly for parts of the tour that we actually renamed our perpetually nagging, faithful old friend 'The Coldplay Cloud'.

Still, there were always some sunny moments to fall back on. One or two came courtesy of Wayne Kwiat, a twenty-something septic (see glossary – sorry Wayne) lampy who joined us for the entirety of our *Viva* extravaganza. Proving without doubt the theory that Coldplay's immediate environment is an all-inclusive land bristling with golden opportunity, this young chap who, like Swayze, Bacon and Travolta before him, was just a regular American kid that loved to dance, went from fucking around offstage in front of us lot with a bit of Jay-Z and our Maglites for backup to being the spotlit star of the pre-show, break-dancing, sweeping up with a broom and – yes – *body-popping* right out on the catwalk to a tour total of 2.75 million Coldplay fans. Moral: If you're going to show off your moves, make sure you do it when Chris Martin's dad's watching.

The first actual stadium show we did was at Stockholm's Olympiastadion, the really old one built for the 1912 Olympics. At a maximum capacity of about 30,000 it wasn't the biggest, but had a lovely vibe to it that newer, larger gaffs can't match. (Will Champion, being a fan of all sport and its history, seemed especially enchanted to be there.) We had an exciting night, it being our first real taste of proper outdoor bigness. Doing a stadium is a bit like working in an arena without a roof: same gig-friendly shape but with a major difference in the sheer scale of the thing, which doesn't really hit you until the crowd start to file in and you realise how tiny and far away the people sat at the back look. Not to mention the sudden realisation that, because there's lots more voices to sing it, the 'Viva' football chant just got even louder.

To be honest, although it sounds daft, I've no idea what the actual *Viva* stadium shows were like really. My axe bunker was more isolated than before due to spatial issues and I had a massive gantry right up the middle of it, like a tree growing through the kitchen of an old farmhouse, which effectively kept me six feet back from the stage edge. As a result, I couldn't really see much besides Jonny and his guitar unless I went up the steps towards the band or out wide to the wings. Maybe next time I'll ask for a periscope.

After Stockholm came Hanover, a big, fuck-off modern venue with a larger capacity and a more gigantic feel to it. The first stadium that really blew us away as we looked out at it from the stage, it just seemed like the craziest, hugest, most rock 'n' roll thing in the world, even to eyes that had become fairly accustomed to the sight of large gigs over the years, as if we were old mariners agape at the sight of an approaching wave to end all waves. 'How could this thing get any bigger?' we all wondered. I mean, it's a good job a lot of us have built up to this madness from pubs, through clubs, theatres, arenas and sheds; if you just showed up at a stadium first-off with no run-up it'd probably knock you over. A bit like the front curtain nearly did to Chris Martin when it landed on his head that very same night. Holy moly.

It's hard to believe this kind of stuff when it happens simply because it totally out-Taps the Tap, but honestly, he was just leaning into the opening lines of 'Violet Hill' right after the band's big instrumental 'Life in Technicolour' overture when the 'kabuki' – a big, black, droppable gauzey drape that hangs on a truss and works fine when there's no wind whatsoever – blew inwards, fell badly and went 'plop', all over him, the microphones and Jonny's pedal board as well. Fucking hell, as my carpentry teacher once said when I broke the belt sander, aged thirteen. This is where stage-based crew really earn their stripes, as long as it wasn't their fault the shit happened in the first place; you've got a guitar in one hand, a suddenly crumpled mic stand in the other, picks all over the floor, an effects cue coming up and a bit of heavy black cloth covering all the pedals with 40,000 people in front of you while other roadies try to help the lead singer fight his way out of what now looks like a recently collapsed tent. Hilarious weeks later, but not at all on the night.

There's no shortage of comic stuff like this that happens around bands and their crews, but the bigger things get the more daft the gaffes seem to sound. For instance, rather like when I ran out of diesel back in Portsmouth on an early *Parachutes* gig and had to ask the band to get out and push, the cargo plane hauling all our gear got hemmed into a corner one morning at an international high-profile cargo terminal right at the front of the whole tour. After a quick coffee, a fag and a natter with the airport's chief of staff our trusty, never-say-die head of freight managed to get the whole thing yanked out with massive chains attached to great big trucks. When people say things like 'The show must go on', this is the kind of thing they're talking about. If our man hadn't done what he did, we'd have completely missed the gig in Barcelona, or been doing it with rented ukuleles.

Anyway, the kabuki went away after that, much to everyone's relief. Dusseldorf's LTU Arena (another proper stadium) and Munich's Reitstadion Riem (an outdoor arena with trees round the top) flew by, leading us nicely into a show at the infamous Stadio Friuli, home of well-known northern Italian soccer club Udinese.

Crumbling and worn, this knackered old 1970s warhorse is an alarming, gnarly place to arrive in. Ageing concrete, peeling yellow paintwork, threadbare surfaces, nasty security devices such as razor-sharp terrace fencing and – best of all – a rock-hard, empty moat that encircles the pitch all give the impression that if you've come here looking for trouble, you're going to bloody well get it. Luckily for us, the crowd, weather and concert itself were all made of vintage Italian stuff. It was sexy, it was romantic and, above all, it was noisy as fuck. We were on our way.

Next were Switzerland (where they don't call for encores, but wiggle their hands and go 'WOOOOOO' instead – always spooky and even more so in a packed stadium), Spain and France, where the kids screamed as soon as the doors opened and didn't let up until way after Coldplay's last firework went off. Nijmegen – possibly pronounced 'Nymeggun', 'Nuimiggin' or even 'No, McGinn' depending on one's orientation and frame of mind – was our final Euro town. After our second night we ran for the beers and sped straight through the night to Calais where, if you remember, we unearthed our second ever bus stowaway and, unbelievably, got on the boat for home the next morning.

I say 'unbelievably' because here we were, heading back to the UK for the last week of the whole bloody thing. We've never really ended a big tour on home turf, it's always Mexico or Japan or somewhere, which feels completely different. I mean, no Auntie Mabel on the guest list for a start. This might sound silly, but having people you know along always makes you more uptight, even as a roadie, so multiply that by who knows how many and you might just get an idea how tense Coldplay could be feeling as they get ready to hit the *really* big time on their own soil.

Wait a minute, though. Has anyone the slightest idea how totally, certifiably unhinged everyone on the *Viva* tour is feeling by this point? How much we want to see a different face? Hear a different song? Or no music at all? Or how hallucinatory and utterly brain-dead, sleep-deprived bananas most of us are going? Don't misread me, it's a cool trip, filled with feelings, sights and jokes that most civilians mightn't get near in a lifetime, but still. We're fucked. People start unravelling with the end in sight; like they say, there's many a slip twixt cup and lip, and the last bit of *Viva* saw its fair share of broken china. Post-show bus benders and the resulting hangovers became way more commonplace in many departments and the atmosphere wasn't always pretty; shouting matches, which could be about anything from a dodgy comment to someone's choice of music, accompanied some completely insane levels of imbibement in bars and back lounges all across Europe. One roadie got so hammered he even puked on his own flight case, while some succumbed to mental pressures of a darker kind that we won't discuss here; it was all symptomatic of a wider malaise though, almost as if everyone was desperate to let go of the reins after so long, but knew they couldn't. I definitely got more moody as the pressure and tiredness mounted and the enormity of the two Wembley shows loomed. Everyone, from the bottom to the top, was absolutely shattered but still racing like crazy, running on empty tanks, caffeine, whatever stamina they'd got left and a bit of pure nervous energy. In the end, it was the only way to keep going. Heads down for the home straight.

Manchester gave us an ecstatic reception (although a rogue, allegedly Scouse, contingent also gave Neill and security honcho Frosty a bit of physical abuse on the way back from the 'C' stage) and we boarded a fast Seacat to Phoenix Park, Dublin, for our last green-fielder where the emerald audience were, as ever, completely lovely and sent us all off to Scotland with a spring in our step.

Glasgow was glorious, but far from full. A bit of a shock this, so near to the end, especially since Coldplay and Scotland have always enjoyed such a happy, healthy relationship, but there you go. You can't sell 'em all. The empty spaces were filled with big, posh, lit-up *Viva* balloons and everyone just got on with the show, then it was back on the bus for a few beers, a kip and . . .

I'm really glad I went home the night before our first Wembley. I was lucky to have the choice – most crew didn't. It almost felt normal to sleep in my own bed, get up, kiss the missus and the bairn goodbye then go to work on the Tube with all the commuters and schoolkids doing what they do all year round, when I was so far removed from their reality it made me a bit numb to be near it. But it felt good too, like those nights way back when you stayed out so late that everyone was heading for the office just as you were weaving your way homeward, still on a buzz, as Supergrass might have said at the time. It was a sunny morning over London, just like Live Aid day nearly 25 years before, with crisscross vapour trails way up high in the nice blue sky. Excitement, fear and glee all tugged at me as the train went overground out of Finchley Road. A few more minutes of day-dreaming and then . . . fuck me, there it was.

All right, so it's not the same crumpled old stadium where I watched Mick Jagger get upstaged by the World Cup back in 1990, not even close. It's got new fancy red seats. It's clean. It's safe. And it's got a big, silly arch on top that makes it look like a massive grocery basket with a handle. But who cares? It's Wembley.

That's W-E-M-B-L-E-Y. And not even the arena, sat right next door, where we started, which now looks tiny, but (sing it): WEM-BER-LEEE, WEM-BERLEE! Wembley Stadium! Where they play the FA Cup Final!

Let's not piss about. Wembley is the fucking daddy. You can see it from Pluto. Even Americans have heard of it, right? And, if you're European or, more specifically, British and – particularly – an English football or rock 'n' roll lover it's knitted into your psyche from such a young age that there's just no escape. It's emblematic of a billion childhood dreams. Young footballers, musicians and more besides all imagine their full-grown selves playing for a packed house at Wembley Stadium (I know I did) though in truth most of us will never even get to *attend* a game or a show there, never mind be involved in any way. With that in mind, permit me a little enjoyment as I take a deep breath and stride purposefully, fearfully, respectfully up the quarter-mile drag they call Olympic Way, right into the belly of the beast.

It's one to savour, this. If you've actually been arsed to plough through the whole 200-odd pages of this book so far, then: (a) I salute you; and (b) you'll know what this little walk means to me. I mean, I didn't hang about smelling the roses, I had to get to work, but I made sure to look around and remember it forever as I passed the new burger vans and a few small groups of people, some on their way to the office, some calling the oft-recited line 'Tickets for Coldplay, buy or sell', some just out early, walking the dog. I found the entrance, walked past security – proudly showing my pass as if it was a *Jim'll Fix It* badge – then down a ramp, up another, through the scaffolding and . . . whoa. Just look at that.

Like I said about Stockholm, stadiums don't seem that much bigger than arenas when you're standing on the stage and the gaff's empty; it's when the place fills up you really feel it. But being in the middle of this daft, wonderful place at 10 a.m. is like landing on the moon mixed with walking into your favourite pub. There's so much familiarity all around (same stage, same gear) and yet it's just as surreal as fuck. These moments can't last though. Right before you float away up your own inflated arse, another roadie walks by, says good morning and farts, or belches, or starts hammering a nail in and reminds you what you're there for and how much you fancy a bacon sandwich. So, it's off the stage again and a quick walk down to catering.

Vibes and victuals taken care of, I head back for what's essentially the same day's work as usual but with a huge side order of happy anticipation and first-night nerves, a bit like the last day of term and the first day of school all rolled into one. You know how our gig goes up by now so I won't bore you; the atmosphere among the crew, though, is noticeably different. Perhaps a little more careful, a little more deliberate, just pushing things into a slightly more serious place. Or perhaps everyone's just pretending to be cool and is really shitting it underneath and/or really hungover. Mystic has his trademark 'End of Tour Cold', which makes things a lot quieter and a bit less fun, for a start. He's usually the chatty, lovely, happy one bustling from spot to spot with a nice word for everyone. Not today. The poor fucker looks and sounds like Jim Royle after a rare sprint for the bus.

Still, on the show must go. And just before lunchtime – earlier than usual so Jay-Z, Girls Aloud and White Lies can get a decent run at it – the show shows up.

It's good to see the band looking as chuffed and blown away to be here as I'm feeling. There've been a few moments like this down the years; Red Rocks was one and their first sell-out at Brixton was another, but today Coldplay walk out onto their huge set in shades, smiling and staying stuff like 'wow' and 'can you believe it' in hushed tones, like a bunch of kids that got given the key to the chocolate factory and are still amazed, even though they totally earned it and it's theirs to keep for the next two nights at least. Chats had, plans made, ideas shared, a few new bits tried and that's it, soundcheck done. Cover it all up and wait for night to come. Oh, please, please let it go well.

While we're here, let's throw in a bit of credit to our stage manager Kurt Wagner and all the other onstage crew. Ours wasn't the biggest main stage area to ever grace a stadium – it was narrow front to back, which didn't leave the other Wembley acts much room to play with. It took a feat of some ingenuity to get all four bands and their rock star gear on and off this platform efficiently and without people feeling too squeezed during their respective shows. But everyone seemed to play nicely and no toys flew out of any prams that I noticed, which means either: (a) I'm living in a world of my own; or (b) there's hope for showbiz yet. Either way, the gang did a great job.

So, what to do? String some guitars? Have a kip on an empty flight case? (The tour buses have all gone by now.) Wander about? Go to catering again? Eat more, drink extra tea? I'm pacing about, basically, waiting for my friends and family to call up saying, 'We're in, can you come and say hello?'

No! Leave me alone! I'm too busy pacing about!

As it was, the local security at both Wembley shows made any sort of movement – pacing or otherwise – a bit more tricky than usual by taking it all to extremes. There were bouncers *everywhere*. You couldn't watch Girls Aloud by ducking under the catwalk, but you could do from up on the raised platforms, in full view of the audience. You couldn't get to your mum in Block 104 without the right extra wristband – 'Access All Areas' seemed to go out of the window as a concept once the doors were open – but you could give your dad a leg up onto the side of the stage if you 'had a word' with the right bloke, waved your laminate and smiled a bit. You could only use the stage-side plastic portaloos if you were a pop star . . . actually, this one's probably fair enough when you think about it. If I was Cheryl Cole I doubt I'd feel like running off for a quick slash mid-show if I suspected Hoppy or Bash had just taken a big poo in there and used up all the bog roll. Still, the whole thing was sort of a bit strict-parenty, right down to the huge message on a big blue lit-up sign high up above the seats at the back encouraging punters to 'plan enough time for the journey home'. What about 'Don't forget to clean your teeth' as well, while you're at it?

Anyway, what often happens with huge, portentous shows like these where expectation is running as high as a bad fever is that the first night rocks like a bastard and the final show's a damp squib. I wouldn't go as far as to say this was reversed for Coldplay at Wembley – as I've pointed out before, these lads' idea of a 'damp squib' and everyone else's don't really match and from a fan's perspective I doubt they're ever disappointing – but I reckon it's fair to say, without fear of the sack, that some nights it's a gig, other nights it's something else.

The first night was definitely a gig. Jonny's guitar sound wasn't quite right for a start – my fault really, I thought the distortion we were hearing through our in-ears was a monitoring thing when, as I discovered the following day, it was just a worn-out valve in one of his amps. Yeah, I should have swapped to the spare Marshall mid-show, but the word from out front was that all was well so we stuck with it as it was. (It wasn't a *bad* sound, just a bit more *metal*, you know?) There was a sense about the whole performance of just getting through it really, sort of dealing with your nerves and not making too many mistakes, though that might just have been me.

The second night, however, was firmly in the 'something else' category, no question about it.

I began the day in my own bed, covered in cards, gifts and my nearly-three-year-old daughter, who seemed way more excited than I was about the fact it was my 44th birthday. (I don't think she really understood the 44th bit – a birthday's a birthday though, right?) It was a lovely way to start the last day of a massive tour but all the same I couldn't help thinking about getting my arse back out to Wembley, seeing what was up with that pesky amp and giving Jonny Buckland the best guitar sound he, or anyone else for that matter, had ever heard. Still, there was fun to be had opening gifts and rolling around the bed scoffing my lovely home-baked guitar-shaped cake, which was pink and had that funny, rubbery liquorice-type stuff for strings. No, I didn't count them, but I'm sure there were six, not seven or five, and I left home in a happy, if trepidatious sort of mood.

Same journey. Almost like going to work. Same venue. Same everything, but . . . no, not the same at all. Something in the air, a sense of birthday fun, I guess. No soundcheck, so Paul, Bash and me backed lampy girl/Joan Jett wannabe Marta Iwan on a semi-rehearsed, partly brilliant, empty-stadium mangle of 'I Love Rock 'n' Roll', which Andy 'Twinkle' Bramley was meant to sing backing vocals on too but only got to hear as he was walking down from the nearby hotel. Shame, but still, I haven't had so much fun since playing 'Purple Rain' on guitar at a Coldplay line check, centre stage at First Avenue, Minneapolis (where they filmed *Purple Rain* – the 1984 Prince film – come on, keep up!).

Adding to the jollity, Hop gave me a splendid birthday gift, wrapped in yesterday's set list and held fast with red electrical tape. I was delighted – it was the *Jackie* magazine 70s compilation CD: three discs packed with classics such as The Osmond's 'Crazy Horses', 'Love Me for a Reason' and, best of all, 'Puppy Love', which Tony Smith blasted for me specially, really fucking loud, out of the PA, almost making me feel a bit weepy. Never mind it being Wembley Stadium, the last gig *and* my birthday; I'd seriously forgotten how much I really loved Donny.

Back in the chapter called 'Gig Day' – in case anyone actually managed to plough through it – you might recall me describing the 'electrical crackles in the air' before a show, or something like that. Well, imagine a normal gig and multiply it by fifty – that's what it feels like backstage on the day of your final turn at arguably the biggest, most famous rock 'n' roll venue in the world. There were way more people around for a start – all Coldplay's friends and families were there and both Jay-Z and Girls Aloud had pretty sizeable entourages in tow including friends, make-up people, backing musicians and crew. (Quite a few parents even had their babies and toddlers with them, adding to the oddness of it all.) Catering was right off the main corridor and about as active as it ever gets; Heidi 'Queen Of Nosh' Varah tells me they made 435 evening meals that day, surely a world record of some sort, especially since she was about seven months pregnant at the time!

The atmosphere around the backstage area wasn't bad at all, despite the craziness. Everyone was up for it, it was nice, it was happy, lots of hugs and 'I'm gonna miss you's going on. It was just very tense and very busy, chock-a-block with little huddles of people either bustling around looking serious and uptight (at work) or hanging out chatting (not at work in the slightest).

Even the guest list turned out to be an art form in itself. It took Marguerite's new assistant Nicole and a small family of elves most of the working day to get all the tickets into envelopes, sitting on the floor surrounded by names and a big, big hat (nearly 800 comps were dished out, possibly another record). There was also the usual smattering of celebs, who, as we've said, you never quite get used to the sight of. They always look smaller in real life too, unless it's Lennox Lewis, of course.

I've been called the greatest roadie in the world once or twice over the years, which is nice, but obviously bollocks. I'll tell you this though, I felt like Jesus Christ himself as, with about an hour to go before the show, I came upon PA technician Owen McCauley who was laying prostrate in the crew room having, unbeknown to me, sprained his ankle really badly in some PA-related incident a couple of days before. Thinking he was just a bit knackered and pissed off, I offered a friendly 'Hey pal, what's up?' playfully punctuated by a firm, friendly squeeze of the lower leg.

In his defence, he neither screamed nor called me a bastard. But I wouldn't necessarily say he took it like a man, either. The alarming moan/whimper the poor lad issued forth (he sort of did both at once) sounded like it came from a place of true suffering and would have totally spoiled my day had I not then bumped into him walking around normally a few minutes later, saying, 'What did you do, McGoo? I'm healed!' Apparently something went click and I'm hoping, since I've so far not been sent any sort of bill, that he's well on the way to a full recovery. And that he thinks I'm some kind of latent roadie Derren Brown, as well.

Right before show time, everyone gets called into the Friends and Family room for the customary end-of-tour awards ceremony, hosted by Her Majesty (an impersonator, though some of the Americans weren't too sure) and what looked like the Duke of Wellington (Phil Harvey). We all got little butterfly-shaped medals on red ribbons for such varied distinctions as 'Whitest Smile' and 'Maddest Axeman', though I think the finest comment of all was received by Chris 'Woody' Wood as he knelt before his queen, looking for all the world like a humble roadie Gandalf. As is often the way on these occasions, Will Champion couldn't resist chipping in with a line he must have been saving for years: 'This must be, what, your twelfth monarch?'

So. Final changeover. Wayne's last dance. Lights go down. The crowd screams . . . and it pours. Absolute fucking buckets. Straight down like stair rods, as your grandad used to say, all over the audience and the front of the stage, pedal boards, mic stands, Rich Ellis and all the camera boys in the pit, my mum, the lot. Thank heavens it wasn't blowing inwards towards the drums and amps too or we'd have had some big problems. We got a bit of warning, a few spits and spots during line check, so at least the essentials got covered up but still, here come Coldplay, striding out, sparklers aloft into the biggest deluge since Abu Dhabi. Poor sods, I thought. On their last night, as well. What rotten luck.

But it was perfect. Drenched as their fans, drowned like rats, the band ripped into the final UK *Viva* set like it was their last day on earth. Guy has said since that quite often bad weather during shows will bond the four of them together and glue the audience to the performance better than anything; this was never truer than on the night of Saturday 19 September 2009, though of course there was a downside. The rain was so thick, wet and heavy it seemed to wrap a soggy blanket round Jonny's guitars, making them sound and feel as dead as a doornail, especially during the catwalk section of 'In My Place', which went from chimey to slimey in a matter of seconds. We swapped Blacky out for Sunny during the dark moment before 'Glass of Water' and he was away again, but it was a sorry sight that greeted me when I got back down to my lit-up axeworld; the damn thing had got so wet the body had started to dapple with white blotches and the strings, neck and bridge felt like something we'd fished out of the bloody river. I had to act fast – he'd be needing this guitar again pretty soon and for a lot of the rest of the gig too so, between pressing buttons for effects cues and peering out through the letterbox to see how he was getting on, I wiped down the instrument and cleaned each string with Fast Fret. Hey presto, new guitar! I was chuffed. But not as chuffed as I was about Owen's ankle.

The rain stopped after a few tunes but it had done its job. 'Yellow' – with more balloons than there were stars in its lyrics – puffed up its chest, suddenly reminding me why I'd called it a 'catchy fucker' in the first place, all those years ago. The whole show sped by like a freight train, unstoppable and unbeatable. As I said, I never get to see Coldplay gigs anyway, but from a professional point of view it was some piece of hard committed work everyone turned in that night, from Chris, Jonny, Guy and Will right through to the roadies on the stage doing the set moves, the pristine RF quality, even down to the last confetti blast which worked better than it ever had on the whole tour, mirroring the earlier rainfall with its own lovely, multicoloured shower.

But best of all, Jonny came down for his little break/sip of water/shirt change/wipe down/body spray (Tiff would show up each night to help with this – there are limits!) after the 'B' Stage interlude and said, almost shouting, 'Great sound, Matt. Best ever. Thanks.'

I could hardly speak, but managed, 'I'm gonna miss this.'

To which he replied, 'Me too. Let's go and do Siberia!'

With that and a quick, slightly-too-fragrant hug, he was gone, back out there to slam into 'Viva La Vida' for the last time. Maybe I'll let him off for forgetting my birthday after all . . .

As I stood at the top of the steps, freshly painted Reddy in hand, waiting for that last, mid-song 'Scientist' guitar change, I gazed for a moment at the vast audience, the monster view and the huge *War Of The Worlds* delay towers and wondered – poetically – who's more wowed, us or the crowd? I didn't feel scared any more, just relieved. And though I was still way out to sea, I didn't feel quite so out of my depth either. Wembley Stadium, the biggest, baddest, bossest venue of them all, stretched up and away all around me, seeming to say:

'Matt McGinn. You're still a bit too small!'

Well, yeah. Maybe. But at last I knew what I was doing there.

GLOSSARY

Aftershow: Party after a show, often at the venue, or close by. Social whirl akin to a village fete with booze, during which lampies chum down with record execs and everyone's your mate. (Or, a chance for glamour seekers who missed the gig to continue drinking for nothing and get cornered by terrifying, drug-crazed roadies after most sane people have fucked off. And there aren't any cabs left either.)

Amp: Boxy, electronic device with knobs which, when connected to a speaker, will make anything musical put through it sound amazing. Or like baying, wet, poorly hounds, depending.

Axe: Guitar, if you're a bit of a twat.

Backline: Anything a group uses onstage, i.e. drums, amps, guitars, pianos etc. The first touring department to reach the bar in any situation, and – with others – the closest team to the actual band onstage during the show. Fucking frontline, more like.

Balalaika: Triangular, guitar-esque instrument from old Russia. 'Let me hear your balalaikas ringin' out!' demanded Beatle Paul on 'Back in the USSR', sounding a bit keen and chuckly, almost like he meant something else entirely.

Bassist: Coolest member of most bands, seemingly. Less strings, less stress.

Beck's: The roadie's pal. Post show, backstage or on the bus, nothing else hits the spot quite as hard. Deceptively moreish and thus dangerously potent.

Boom camera: Effective, modern device used for clouting roadies about the head and bashing up their stuff. Like a big crane with a wrecking ball (sorry, camera) at one end and a sadist (cameraman) at the other.

Branston pickle: A sandwich classic, especially with cheese and crisps. The cornerstone of any roadie snack.

Bum note: Bad choice of melodic interval, usually resulting in much chortling among onlookers and listeners. (Check out some old footage of late comedian Les Dawson at the piano for deliberate howlers taken to their comic zenith.)

BVs: Backing vocals.

Carp: Short for carpenter. In civvy street, this term usually means someone who gets up, goes to work, makes stuff out of wood then goes home for supper. On the road, its meaning changes to 'hardest-working, multipurposest dude on the whole damn tour'. Watch carps go as they push gear off trucks in the morning, build stages, sweep stages, *mop* frickin' stages, do set changes during shows, mend everyone's busted-up old shite, pass Matt McGinn his missing guitar, load out after shows until 3 a.m. etc. Give these people a raise! NB, sometimes used as a verb, i.e. 'Is it broken? Can we carp it?'

Clipboard: Essential accessory for hot young thing working at a TV station. See also 'Headphones'.

Cotton pimp: Dodgy name for merchandiser. I daren't Google it.

Crew: Team of professional knobheads at large. Rugby tour/school playground parallels may be evident on close inspection. Not particularly normal.

Delay towers: Tall, gantry-like structures out in the crowd with speakers, lights, screens and Xmas decorations bolted onto them. Not to be confused with Tony Smith's Spanish guest house of the same name.

Downstage: Towards the audience

Drum riser: Little stage for drum kit and drummer. Not everyone uses them – Keith Moon didn't, for instance, preferring to be down on the stage with the others, bless him.

Fast Fret: Spread-on, wipe-off guitar string treatment, sort of like roadie lipstick. Intended as an enabling item for slippery-fingered showy types, but actually cleans strings and fretboards up a treat.

Fender: Possibly the largest, most famous guitar manufacturer in the world, along with Gibson.

Flashman: Fictitious cad. Main protagonist in politically idiosyncratic, historically fascinating book series favoured by me, Jonny Buckland and Anthony 'Chris's Dad' Martin. Cracking!

FOH: Front Of House, or that bit near the middle of the stalls that's fenced off and looks like Cape Canaveral. Lights, sound, you name it, it's all controlled from here, and often affords the best view too; look closely, you might see a film star, or even someone's mum. Just don't throw any beer, though. You will die (well, get chucked out and ruin the gig, at any rate).

Gibson 335: Big old-fashioned 'semi-acoustic' guitar, i.e. it sports electronics but also has 'F' holes like a violin. Imagine Chuck Berry, BB King, Noel Gallagher, Kings of Leon or even Haircut 100 if it helps.

Groupie: Extreme strain of music fan. Follows bands and does whatever they want (blow jobs, laundry, trips to the shop etc.). Google 'Cocksucker Blues', 'Pamela Des Barres' or 'GTO's' for full, amazing picture.

Hangover: Par for the course.

Headphones: See clipboard.

Itinerary: Small book containing daily tour details: hotel addresses, journey times, venue phone numbers etc. Also known, perhaps uncharitably, as 'The Book of Lies'.

Jack, Jack Daniel's: The roadie's enemy. Evil tipple meant for sipping. Often guzzled in error, post Beck's.

Jam [1]: Hip-sounding word for collective, improvised musical invention; or snappy name for a pile of totally irksome old wank, depending on who's doing the jamming. Can be utterly inspirational and produce great songs/musical passages, or may take a wrong turn down the slip road onto Bumwipe Freeway, via its own arse.

Jam (The) [2]: Fantastic band from ages ago. Best elements of punk and mod meet soul and balls-out rock 'n' roll. Right up there with The Clash, despite their total-hair-coolness percentage being a bit lower thanks to a bit of a mullet in the rhythm section.

Jim'll Fix It: 70s and 80s UK primetime TV show, featuring kids' dreams and Jimmy Savile with a cigar. YouTube it!

Keyboard: Anything with lots of keys that isn't a caretaker.

Keyboard Pad [1]: Big sound out of a keyboard . . . Van Halen, 'Jump', etc.

Keyboard Pad [2]: Rick Wakeman's house.

Knobhead: Northern English derogatory expression. Means 'idiot', 'twat', 'arse', 'pillock' and also 'cockhead'.

Label: Record company.

Laminate: Backstage pass made of plastic, worn on 'lanyard' (posh bit of coloured string). Hierarchical by definition. Having 'AAA' written on it means you can go anywhere, 'VIP' means you can't go in the dressing room without the singer's dad, 'WORKING' means you're allowed to clean the bog naked, etc.

Lampy: Beck's drinker with penchant for heights, power and danger. Also doubles as lighting specialist and electrical wizard.

Lead: Pronounced 'Leed', unless you mean some actual metal, this could be used to describe a cable (guitar lead) or as in 'lead guitarist', meaning 'Flash Harry who's doing the showy parts'.

Leckie tape: Electrical tape. Or Stone Roses first album, prior to mastering.

Line [1]: Path followed by noise after source, usually along cables. Destination: Front of House.

Line [2]: Path followed by nose after sauce, usually along tables. Destination: Frontal Lobe.

Loom: Multitude of cables taped together or fed down one tubular bit of black stuff. Really handy but not very interesting. Sometimes called a 'snake' in an attempt to jazz things up a bit.

Maglite: Torch favoured by roadies. Black, preferably, and worn about the belt.

Mixing desk: Big thing with a hundred knobs on for making gigs and records sound nice. Only two of these knobs actually work, 'Volume' and 'Tone', but engineers are paid by the knob, so . . .

Multipin/multicore: Like a 'loom', but even duller.

Muso: Someone too good on their instrument who doesn't like punk rock. Catch-all term for boring musical cockhead.

Noise boys/girls: Collective name for PA crew. This means everyone from the tough lads and lasses who lift amps, push trolleys and hang speakers right through to the sonic wizards who mix the show.

Noisy bus: A noisy bus (because of what's happening on it, not a mechanical fault, hopefully).

Noodle/Noodling: Pissing around aimlessly on an instrument to the annoyance of all and sundry. May result in a hit tune, permanent estrangement from your peers, unplugging or even bullying.

Oilspot: Verb. To leave a roadie behind at a hotel, truck stop, venue etc., accidentally or even on purpose. No fun whatsoever for the oilspottee. May result in a frantic taxi ride or an angry, semi-trouserless sprint after the departing busload of friends/utter bastards.

PA [1]: Public address system. Like a big hi-fi with a live band's sound going through it. Expansive, collective term that encompasses microphones, cables, amps, speakers, effects, mixing desks, monitors, Chris Wood's suit of armour, etc.

PA [2]: Personal assistant. Extremely useful, scurrying crew member, usually seen backstage carrying multiple phones and radios while holding three conversations at once. Rarely heard to utter the words 'No, sorry, it can't be done', despite overwhelming desire to scream 'Fuck off, I'm busy!'

PDs: Per diem. Funny Latin name (meaning 'for each day') for roadies' pocket money, paid by employers. Distributed regularly in enveloped, cash chunks throughout the tour's duration. Usually sent home to the family, to top up the housekeeping.

Peage: French pay-as-you-go motorway, where it's apparently illegal to run out of gas. This happened to me in a tour van once, resulting in a retrospectively hilarious 'Move the vehicle, Monsieur!' – 'We can't!' face-off.

Plectrum: Hand-held plastic fingernail-type device used for guitar strumming.

Pledge/Mr Sheen: Waxy spray-on polish for furniture/tour bus worktops, etc. Not really usable on posh guitars though – get some proper stuff!

Pompadour: 50s hairdo (similar to quiff).

Promo: Any sort of promotional duties e.g. magazine interviews, TV appearances, radio etc. Usually seen as a drag but absolutely necessary and sometimes fun.

Pussy pass: Given out to female audience members by lustful roadies, sometimes on a particularly sleazy band's behalf. Such a naff old term it's not even in the book.

Real estate: Universal roadie term meaning precious space in which he/she is going to be setting up all their stuff. A major issue at festivals, particularly if you're further down the bill and the big groups' crews have taken up all the room already and are refusing to move.

Riff: Short musical figure cool enough to repeat over and over . . . hopefully (e.g. that nagging, buzzy-bee guitar part that runs through 'I Can't Get No Satisfaction').

Rigger: Crazy bastard who's acting normal, despite hanging off a skyhook by the shorts for part of the day. Often to be found in extreme circumstances during downtime, e.g. up a mountain, down a deep hole, near large fires etc.

Roadie: Man/woman in black T-shirt and blue jeans who does stuff for a group. Often thirsty. (That's it . . . you don't need to read the book.)

Routing: Something the average roadie should never even ponder. Unless you're a driver or in some form of management there's fuck all you can do about where you're going and in what daft order, so don't do it to yourself. You'll only get upset.

Royalty: Something from the past that keeps generating dough.

Septic: English rhyming slang for Yank, i.e. 'Septic tank'.

Set list: Crucial piece of white A4 showing running order of songs for gig. Not used by all bands but usually well worth having on any big night (although accidentally putting one wrong list out for just the drummer could lead to badness, hilarity and much more besides).

Shredding: Showing off, doing solos, really fast. Like noodling but speeded up and given 'purpose'.

Signal path: Route followed by sound to any final point, e.g. from a guitar all the way – via any effects devices, etc. – to whatever amplifier/speaker it's plugged into.

Snare drum: The small one in the middle between the drummer's knees that you can't see and he/she keeps on hitting, over and over. So called because it has a few wires attached to the bottom skin. Goes along through most rock songs and sounds a bit military, like the Boys Brigade.

Speaker: Loud thing in a cabinet (or 'cab'). Makes mere bands seem like Norse Gods when working correctly. Black, preferably.

Stage left: Left as you look out from onstage.

Stage right: You getting it?

Stringfellows: Cheesy, rude old London nightclub.

Tech: Roadie in denial.

Theremin: Strange, radio-like device used to generate odd noises. Sounds a bit like a bowed saw, in the right hands (of which there aren't a lot).

Thinline Telecaster: Type of vintage Fender axe favoured by our own JB. Sweet!

Toilet circuit: British concert trail taking in a selection of celebrated small, rough-and-ready dives, often set up in seedy little boozers and/or their back rooms. Scene of either excitement or desolation, depending on career curve/punter quota. See 'Tunbridge Wells'.

Tunbridge Wells: Posh hometown of amazingly incongruous small 'toilet' venue The Forum, actually built inside an old bog in the woods.

Upstage: Away from the audience.

Vidiot: Comic but slightly barbed and unreasonable term meaning anyone who has anything to do with cameras, screens, TV etc. Occasionally deserved but often a bit rich, particularly coming from some of the crustacea you sometimes hear using it.

Wedge [1]: Speaker pointing at band, for sound monitoring.

Wedge [2]: Wad of cash, around 1988.

Wedge [3]: Simon Le Bon/Diana Spencer hairdo, early 80s.

Wedge [4]: Wooden chock for a door or whatever.

Wedge (The) [5]: U2 guitarist . . . sorry. That's enough!

FURTHER READING

Psychotic Reactions and Carburettor Dung (Lester Bangs, Serpent's Tail, 2001)

Rock Dreams (Nick Cohn, Kathrin Muir & Guy Peelaert, Taschen, 2003)

The Love You Make (Peter Brown, New American Library, 2002)

U2: At the End of the World (Bill Flanagan, Bantam Books, 1996)

A Journey Through America with the Rolling Stones (Robert Greenfield, Helter Skelter, 1974)

The Jam: A Beat Concerto (Paulo Hewitt, Boxtree, 1996)

Crazy from the Heat (David Lee Roth, Ebury, 1998)

Cider With Roadies (Stuart Maconie, Ebury, 2004)

Before I Get Old: The Story of the Who (Dave Marsh, Plexus,1989)

Music Scene Annual 1975

NME review of re-released Jam singles (Danny Baker, 1982)

INDEX